MOVING FROM
BITTERNESS TO
BETTERMENT
SURVIVING THE PAIN OF ABUSE

EVELYN M. JOHNSON

MOVING FROM
BITTERNESS TO
BETTERMENT
SURVIVING THE PAIN OF ABUSE

EVELYN M. JOHNSON

LOWBAR
PUBLISHING COMPANY

905 South Douglas Avenue • Nashville, Tennessee 37204
Phone: 615-972-2842
E-mail: Lowbarpublishingcompany@gmail.com
Web site: www.Lowbarbookstore.com

Printed in the United States of America
LOWBAR PUBLISHING COMPANY

ISBN: 978-0-9886237-7-4
Nashville, Tennessee 37204

615-972-2842
E-mail: Lowbarpublishingcompany@gmail.com
Web site: www.Lowbarbookstore.com

For additional information, workshops, and seminars, here is how you may contact the author:
Evelyn M. Johnson revej2003@yahoo.com

Copy Editor: David Pollitt
Graphic and Cover Design: Tunisa Rice
Layout Artist: Norah S. Branch

Table of Contents

Dedication

This book is dedicated to the memory of my *Abuelita,* who loved me like no one here on earth ever loved me. She was an example of what a strong woman should be. She was an example of what a caring woman should be; she was an example of a woman who stood her ground. Throughout my life, as I was taking note of my childhood, teenage years and adult life, the image of her sweet face and little voice were very present. My wish for eternity is that the first person I see in heaven will be Jesus, then my grandmother, and that we will forever together worship and praise God singing and dancing. The things that happened to me were not your fault—thank you for taking care of me and loving me so—*Descansa en paz abuelita!* (R.I.P. Abuelita!).

Acknowledgments

First, I give thanks to God for being my creator, provider, and giver of gifts. These gifts I talk about are spiritual gifts; mainly faith, discernment, wisdom, knowledge, the gift of helps, then the human gifts, which I call talents: teaching, writing, reading, editing, proofreading, typing, and researching. If it were not for the LORD, I would not have a story to tell. For, it was He who breathed the breath of life into my being and put me in places where I experienced what I experienced that I may bless others. When I thought about what I went through as being horrible, I thought about it as being for my good. I can safely and peacefully write about my experiences without guilt, shame, remorse, or ill feelings toward anyone. This is God's story, not mine.

Although I started years ago—approximately thirty-five years ago— to write this book, it was not until recently after many trials and tribulations and hindrances that I was ready to complete this work, making it my second instead of my first or third book. It seems funny, right? However, there is a time and a place for everything, especially when we move in God's time. I was moving on my own time and getting nowhere. You see, in order for me to complete this book, I had to be in the right frame of mind. Writing *Pleas, Praises and Promises* first brought me to this point where un-forgiveness is no longer part of my life. I had to look at people with both my spiritual eyes as well as with my eyes of understanding in order to move from bitterness to betterment. The Lord works in mysterious ways; yet, eventually, He reveals all to those who wait upon His revelation. Thank You, Lord, for the gifts, wisdom, and patience that You have showered upon me.

I thank my beloved husband, Arthur, who does not really know this; but, well, he knows SOME of it; he is in Christ, and he has been my calm during and after the storms. While I have been hyper, he has been laid back. We are both strong in different ways. He has supported and encouraged me throughout all my endeavors. He is a good model of a Christian man, husband, father and grandfather, friend, and family member. Through my interaction with him, I have learned to let "certain" things slide off my shoulders. Every now and then in a carefully thought-out, calm voice, he says, *"Isn't it time for you to get back to your writing?"* OR *"Isn't it time for you to get back to your school work?"* It's funny that he would say this just at the same time when I am getting ready to "get back" into what I had temporarily stopped doing. I thank you, Art, for backing up your "wuwy" wife (Art's pet name for me); and continuing to believe in me all these years.

I am thanking my newfound friend and sister in Christ, Pastor Jodi L. Serino-Barbour, author of *To God be the Glory,* whose excitement over this second work motivated me to pound on the keyboard at a faster speed than originally intended: a prayer warrior and Scripture-loving, anointed vessel of God who can do according to her Scripture and mine, "all things through Christ who strengthens" (Philippians 4:13).

A thank you shout-out—to my publisher, Black Essence Award winner Calvin C. Barlow, Jr., President and Publisher of Lowbar Publishing Company! Pastor Barlow has been there in cyberspace to answer my many questions while not pushing me to finish this work. He merely told me months ago, whenever I am ready; and he left it at that. He sent no bothersome e-mails and made no disturbing calls; he was just patient with me. Thank you, Pastor Barlow. (By the way, writers, if you are looking for a reasonably priced publishing company, look no further. His is it!)

To the anointed pastor of Bethel African Methodist Episcopal Church in Hampton, Virginia, great saxophonist and producer of the CD, "Hymns in the Key of Glory"—my pastor, The Reverend André Pierre Jefferson, Sr., M.Div., who always sees the best in me—always pumping me up and telling me how smart I am.... A HUGE thank you to you, Pastor J!

To my friend since 1989 and prayer partner since 2001, Harry Crewe, thank you for your continued encouragement. No matter how pressed or stressed I get, you always say, *"God is blessing."* Thank you for your continued support and well wishes.

To my friend, book reviewer, and champion builder—Motivational Speaker Lakeisha McKnight of Lakeisha McKnight Enterprises (LME), thank you for your wonderful review of my first book, *Pleas, Praises and Promises* and thank you for all your encouraging videos and uplifting messages. May God's name be praised for your continued success!

To all persons who purchased my first book, *Pleas, Praises and Promises* and to my other brothers and sisters or any family member—if you have prayed for me or in any way had good wishes toward me when I told you that I was writing this book—thank you, and may God continue to bless you and prosper you (3 John 1:2).

Introduction

I don't care if it was sexual, physical, emotional, or spiritual abuse. No matter whom you are or what a person or persons did to you, **YOU** did **NOT** deserve it; and it isn't **YOUR** fault; and you should **NOT** keep it to yourself. I believe, even, if someone mistreats you one time by abusing one's power or authority over you; even, if the person doesn't do it again, that's abuse. It is abuse because you are not benefitting; only he or she is. If that action does not encourage you and makes you feel uncomfortable, then it is wrong; it is abuse. You are physically abused when someone strikes your body in such a way that it causes injury, no matter how small the injury. You are sexually abused when someone touches you inappropriately in any of your private areas without your consent. You are emotionally abused when someone hurts your feelings enough to traumatize you while leaving you with emotional scars. Also, you are spiritually abused when someone attacks your faith, your worship, or your praise—BEEN THERE.

Why do adults keep childhood secrets of bad things that have been done to them? Is it fear? Is it shame? If we divulge our secrets, do we think that we will get blamed for what happened to us or that we won't be liked because of what happened to us? If we do it to protect or defend someone, then why do we do it?—DONE THAT.

When one has been abused, either physically, sexually, emotionally, and spiritually in one or all four of these ways, then how does one continue with one's life, move forward, stop wanting to seek vengeance, and remove all bitterness and un-forgiveness from one's heart, mind, and spirit? How?

I wrote *Moving from Bitterness to Betterment: Surviving the Pain of Abuse* because it is my story of physical, sexual, emotional, and spiritual abuse as a child and into my adult life. My ultimate goal is to help others who have also been victims; and for their own personal reasons, they have never told anyone. Many have lived with fear, shame, and in many cases, guilt.

To the little child inside the adult body who has hidden secrets of childhood molestation and physical, emotional, and spiritual abuse—been unwillingly kissed, inappropriately touched, raped, and who has been struggling alone with nightmares, vengeance, bitterness, and un-forgiveness; this is for **YOU.**

AND to any adult (male OR female) who has offended and still is sexually, physically, emotionally, or spiritually offending any child (female OR male); this is for **YOU.**

And, if you do **NOT** fit into any of these categories, bless **YOU,** but please bless someone else. Help someone else by sharing my story and the Scriptures mentioned later in the story and at the end of the book.

SECTION ONE

Sexual and Physical Abuse

Prologue

There I lie, waiting, anticipating, wondering, *why am I waiting here this way? What is he going to do next? What kind of game is this that is played in the dark?* I, Chanchi, as my *abuelita* (grandmother) called me from the moment she laid eyes on me at the tender age of seven months, lying down on my own twin-sized bed, alone and in my dark room. My mother and her sister went shopping and left me in the care of two trusting men. I confidently skip playfully from the living room to my bedroom; there is nothing to fear because, after all, I am in good care. I have known these men for as long as I can remember.

No sooner than I stop skipping and walk into my bedroom, I hear the whispering voice of one of my sitters, *"acuestate"* ("lie down"). "Lie down." "Am I tired? Is it bedtime"? Those questions race in my mind. I do not utter a word for I know better. I have to be obedient to my elders. The soft *"acuestate"* comes with a gentleness that cannot be resisted. I, Chanchi, lie down as he smoothly pulls my little girl panties down. This is easy for I do not wear pants, just cute little girls' dresses.

Acuestate y espera" (*"Lie down and wait."*) are the words he used, leaving me there curious and confused, remembering the day he sits on the edge of the bathtub in the dark. I have no clue why, except that he asks me to come over to him then draws me close to him, gently pulling my little girl's body toward his middle part but all of a sudden getting interrupted by my *mami's* voice. Had THAT been a game too? And is this waiting in my room in the dark room a part of the same game?

As I lie there in obedience with my little girl undies down and legs spread in position, he quietly reaches for the light switch, turns off the light, and in his soft raspy voice assures me, *"Vengo pronto"* (*"I will be right back."*) I do as I am told. If I am not obedient, then it's the extension cord for me. I am not sure if he will use it on me, but I am terrified because that is what I grew up with—the beating with the extension cord for being disobedient. The extension cord is just one of the means of punishment; another is the belt and yet another

2

is the *"chancleta"* (the house slipper), which is a more lenient way of punishing a disobedient child.

In my family, there is no punishment like *"go to time out."* If that were so, it would not matter much to me for I spent most of my leisure time in my bedroom anyway. During my childhood, my *mami* is very strict with me. She beats me for no reason at all. Two weeks before leaving me with the sitters, she sends me to the store for the first time by myself. I go to the store, but a couple of my friends see me outside and start to talk with me. Well, I stop and talk too. I am so excited about going to the store that I forget that I am to go straight home. No sooner do I walk into the apartment and WHAM! My *mami* starts beating me on my back with the extension cord. I do not get a chance to explain, that yes, I did stop to talk with a couple of friends; but upon realizing that I was going to get into trouble, I said goodbye and rush home. I run so fast that I fall, drop a bag, and fall right on top of a bottle of *Malta Corona* (a carbonated soft drink or unfermented beer that is part of my culture). Upon getting up from the ground, I noticed that the top of my hand was bleeding. I cut my hand with the pieces of the broken bottle. No hospital, no emergency room, no listening ear; just the beating then the well-known cure-all, VapoRub, I guess to soothe the pain. The scar on the hand remains and so does the memory. I do not consider being sent to my room a punishment, but the beating with an extension cord, a house slipper, or a belt, yes. They are the disciplinary methods imposed on me by my mami simply because she feels that I crossed her. If I disagree with her, I get hit; if I look at her cross-eyed, she hits me. She hits me when I do anything to irritate her. She the mom and I am the child. My *mami's* constant physical and emotional abuses leave scars that only forgiveness and time are strong enough to heal. For that is not the only incident. It just happens to occur two weeks before one of the sitters tells me to wait in the dark in my room. I am so confused about the game this sitter is playing because games for me are Hide-and-Go-Seek, Hopscotch, Red Light/ Green Light 1-2-3, Mother May I?, Simon Says, hula hoop, jump rope, tag, running across the yard in the rain, getting wet under the fire hydrant; and board games like checkers, Chinese checkers, Bingo, and Parcheesi;

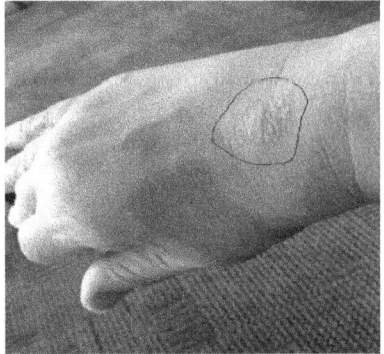

all children's games. This new game is not played outside or indoors with my little friends but on the inside with a grown man. What kind of "game" did this man want me to play with him?

This grown man, whom I trusted; this grown man whom I loved is so familiar to me; since I am an obedient child, then why not do as he tells me to do? Who is this adult who is getting ready to play this unknown game? Who is this grown-up whom I am willing to obey without asking questions? Who? Who?

CHAPTER ONE

. . . .

THE ROLLING STONE (PART 1)

With just a raggedy pillowcase holding three boxer shorts, four button-down shirts, two pairs of pants, two pairs of socks, and the clothes on his back; he runs and runs and runs. As he hurries down the winding road, he finds himself breaking out in a sweat while looking back every few minutes to see if he is being followed. With every beat of his heart he thinks to himself... *"Am I going to get caught? Will I make it?"* He speaks to his other self, the silent self; the self that he knows would not be able to answer him because that other self only exists in the deep wells of his imagination. As he thinks, since he is alone, that if he gets caught with someone else, the penalties of being caught will not be as harsh.

But, he is alone, and alone, he must go forth; and alone, he must face the consequences! Would he get whipped with the dreaded belt? Or beaten with a stick? Or perhaps his hands would be placed on top of a heated stove. Which one? He has endured all these corporal punishments.

For fourteen years, Juan (*Who-on*), a thin, very dark-skinned, blue-eyed, curly haired Puerto Rican teenage boy has been the victim of rejection, physical, mental, and emotional abuse. *"Tu eres tan negro como el carbon y tu pelo tan áspero como un estropajo. Pareciendo como que nadie te va a querer. Nunca llegarás a hacer nada."* ("You are as black as coal and your hair is as rough as a scouring pad".) Looking like that nobody's going to want you. You will never amount to anything.") Those harsh words are thrown at this young man from time to time until the day that he can't take it any longer. He is tired of being abused by the words of one whose responsibility is to unconditionally feed, clothe, protect, and provide a roof over his head—his FATHER! ENOUGH is ENOUGH! There HAS to be some way to escape from this man.

For months, Juan thinks of ways to leave. Where could he go? How and what will he eat? Where will he sleep? Who will be so kind as to take him in? In his mind's eye, he could fly to the United States, but he is too young and penniless. Then all of a sudden, the light bulb lit up! He thought of Mr. and Mrs. Gonzalez, a kind and lonely couple who had shown him favor. *"They'll take me in. Why not? They like me. They know what I go through."* Juan just had to muster enough courage and wait for the right moment to leave his obnoxious home life atmosphere and never go back, but when?

Then, it happens; the opportunity to flee! On August 22, 1916, Hurricane "San Hipólito" sweeps through Puerto Rico with winds of ninety miles per hour. Nonetheless, the storm does not deter him from his purpose. Juan's hopes for a better future are on the other side of abuse. No more bashing, no more beatings, no more heartaches and disappointments. Just a storm away and all his troubles would be washed away! Against the winds and heavy rainfall, this young man runs to what would be his future safe home and loving family. Juan keeps running against the ferocious winds; until two miles away, he reaches the home of this compassionate couple and takes refuge in their arms, not only surviving the hurricane, but overcoming the tormenting images of his abusive past and embracing his new life as a Gonzalez.

There is no mention of Juan's life between the ages of fourteen and the time he married a woman, strangely enough, named Juana (Who-ann-ah). Juana was a heavy-set, light-skinned woman who finished the first grade as a grown up. Her *papi* was a French merchant marine, and her *mami* was a descendant of the *indigenous group the Taínos* (*good people*). Juana was an industrious stay-at-home mom, who made handkerchiefs by hand, ironed other people's clothing, and sold her home-cooked dinners. Juana spoke in a soft tone but underneath that mousy-sounding voice, there is a lot of power.

It is assumed that Juan works odd jobs, helps his new family, and saves some money for a rainy day **AND** for his future. Juan moved to New York City with his wife Juana, became a baker, and a very popular individual, especially with the ladies.

This gets him in trouble. How much can you hide from a wife and nosy neighbors? Well, not enough, because one day he came home from the bakery only to find his clothes on the bed, burned!

Just imagine what his face looked like. Were his eyes bulging out in fear? Were his eyebrows raised in amazement? Was his forehead breaking out in a sweat? That, my friends, we will never know. Did he cheat again? If he did, he was not caught. But, I guess he didn't learn his lesson for he secretly proposed the unacceptable role of a mistress to one of Juana's sisters (who shall remain nameless to protect the names of the living relatives). The thought of betraying her sister was mortifying to her, so she fled from Puerto Rico; and with the money she had saved, she moved to New York City, where, years later, she and Juan met again. But this time, she was married. That did not stop Juan. There were more relatives; one of them being one of his daughters, who will remain nameless.

Juan lived a happy-go-lucky life, in which his friends were of utmost importance to him, especially Jesús (Hay-seus) his partner in the bakery business. Were his partner's opinions and suggestions more important than his wife's? Apparently so; because the moment Jesús suggested a vacation in Puerto Rico, Juan immediately jumped at the chance to go with his buddy. He was so thrilled with the idea that he cashed in his life insurance policy without consulting Juana. No one thought anything was strange or weird about his decision to go with his friend, because they were always together. Where you saw one, you saw the other. So off they went! Four of them went, but only three returned.

As the story is told by his best friend and partner, they were out fishing on a calm and beautiful day in Puerto Rico's longest river, Rio de La Plata (rio means **river** and de la means **of the** and plata means **silver**), when in the blink of an eye, they saw Juan's arms sinking deep down into the water. The others swore up and down that they could not explain how Juan fell overboard! What happened? How was this possible? How could that happen to a great swimmer?

Perhaps, they knew that it mattered not whether Juan was a great swimmer, for Rio de La Plata has a reputation for being a place where bodies disappear. Perhaps this was a set-up. Juan's friend must have known about the insurance money. Where was the money? Had Juan been pushed by one friend and hit over the head by another? If you ask me, this was quite a mystery.

Juan's friends pulled his grotesque and unrecognizable body out of the river. It looked like the crabs had a field day pinching and pulling on it and tearing it apart piece by piece. Because of that tragedy, one of

Juan's grandsons, who is now deceased, never brought himself to eat crabs because in his mind's eye, he actually saw the crabs crawling on top of his grandfather, nibbling at his flesh, tearing it up piece by piece until all he could see is blood and spilled-out guts. The thought of crabs eating his grandfather was appalling to him. His stomach would get queasy and he would turn pale at the mention of the word *crab party*. He died without ever attending a crab party or touching a crab ever again!

What an unfortunate ending for this happy-go-lucky rolling stone. Juan was popular. The man's popularity with the ladies and with friends, then his unfaithfulness to his wife with years of sexual abuse and molestation only led him to that tragic ending in 1964.

"Manteco"

To add insult to injury, Juan's oldest and favorite daughter, *Manteco*, (a nickname with no particular meaning which probably meant "baby" or "sweetie") heard the news of the "drowning" and did not accept it because her father was a great swimmer. She did believe that he had died because she claimed that she saw a sign. Three days before his "accident," *Manteco* had laid down on her bed when out of nowhere, or so she claimed, a white pigeon hovered over her and flew across the room, instantly disappearing into thin air. To her, this was a definite sign that someone had died; and since the pigeon flew really low while nearly skinning her head, she just knew that it was a loved one.

While at Juan's wake, *Manteco* stood by the doorway, grasping on to the door frame while the rest engaged in the dreaded arrangements to deport Juan's body to his homeland. The next moment, when no one was paying attention to her, she let out a loud gasp, then shouted in a raspy yet unrecognizably chilled voice, *"El esta ahi, el esta ahi!,"* (meaning "He is there! He is there!").

Silence filled the room for what seemed the longest two minutes of the entire three hours of the gathering. Until, the moment when her body began to jiggle and twist, arms up in the air, feet stomping, pulling her hair, then she began to shout louder and louder – *"ahi esta, ahi esta, yo se que el no se fue!"* ("There he is, there he is. I knew he wasn't gone!") Clearly, she was delusional for only she saw Juan's ghost; after all, she was Juan's favorite. In light of the circumstances, the family had no other choice but to lock her up at Bellevue Hospital as a mental patient.

Manteco only stayed a few days in the hospital; but tragedy again befell the family as *Manteco's mami* was diagnosed with uterine cancer and died unexpectedly. Her daughters believed that since she was morbidly obese, weighing approximately 500 pounds, the nurse or nurses did not want to deal with her so they injected her with who knows what so that she would die. The suspicions were never confirmed, and the matter was laid to rest along with Juana, who although she had no life insurance, was transported back to her native land. Family and friends took up a collection which helped with the expenses. After all, isn't that what families and friends are for? To help each other in times of need?

Manteco and her family gathered in the same apartment where just months earlier, her father left me there in my room waiting in that awkward position; thinking that I had done something wrong. I was scared to say anything to anyone. What was wrong with my body? Imagine a little girl worried about something being wrong with her body simply because she was left in a position that she shouldn't have been placed in at all? Feelings of inadequacy and shame began to develop inside me. Those feelings continued as I was sexually molested again.

THE WINDOW WATCHER (PART 1)

Here I am again in my room in the dark; one year later. The memory of that night in my room lingers on. The images of me lying there waiting leaves a scar that has not healed in a year's time. These next few times I am lying down getting ready to sleep when all of a sudden (I have always been a light sleeper) I feel the presence of someone there in my room walking towards the window. He stands there staring at who knows what. I keep my eyes closed but wonder what in the world he is doing there and what he is going to do? Again, I keep quiet. Is the same thing going to happen again? Is he going to do like my *abuelo* did and pull down my undies? Is he also going to play a "game"? If so, will he succeed? Or will he also leave me there waiting? Or is it even a game that he wants to play? The first time he enters my room, he quietly stands there staring for a little while, then he leaves. I still do not say anything. One night, I felt him coming in the room, but this time his hand brushes my thigh. I sleep on my belly, so his hand brushes up and down the side of my thigh. I am terrified. I freeze. It feels like my little girl's heart is going to jump out of my chest. I do not like that feeling.

I don't like his hand on my thigh. The voice in my head shouts STOP! Why are you doing this? I don't like this! But my lips were sealed; not a sound was coming out. My eyes shut, not even batting an eyelash. Why? Why was he doing that? Again, I keep quiet.

Who is this man? Who? And how does he get access to my room? What I know about the window watcher is that he is a New York factory worker and a widower with two adult offspring and who by 1954 meets and marries the woman with whom he shares thirty years of his life: Andrea. Why did she marry him? He was not wealthy. He really was not a very talkative, smooth or handsome man. As a matter of fact, he was sixteen (16) years older than she was. It really isn't love at first sight. So what in the world does Andrea see in him?

In the year 1950, Andrea graduated from Central High School in Puerto Rico and was sent to live with her aunt (who shall remain nameless to protect the names of the living relatives) who needs help adjusting in the big city. Andrea did not do anything wrong; it's just that she was the oldest of the daughters and knew how to speak, read, and write in English—a smart woman with dreams and aspirations of becoming a school teacher. But her dreams and aspirations were soon interrupted.

SCARFACE

To interrupt Andrea's dreams, a tall, pale, green-eyed, straight brown-haired, handsome (according to Andrea) and smooth talking man named *Angel (An-hel)* entered her life. As strange as it may sound, at the age of twenty-one, Angel became Andrea's first boyfriend. He was like a refreshing tall glass of lemonade on ice. She had never dated because first, she had spent most of her teenage years sick with asthma; and second, because her mother was very strict about her four daughters dating, even though Andrea was the oldest.

Although Andrea did not know much about him, Angel swept her off her feet, and she immediately fell in love. They secretly met because he was a married man and she was a single woman fresh out of high school. Although a very intelligent woman, Andrea graduated late from high school because her asthma attacks kept her absent from school. During that era, it wasn't common for girls from the islands to speak the English language. Yet, Andrea did!

Dating was a new and wonderful experience for her. Although, their love was a secret love, and their meetings were never exposed. The moment of revelation was at hand for Andrea became pregnant soon after her love encounter. Sex education at her home, as mentioned before, was a taboo subject. Andrea's parents did not talk to their offspring about sex, ESPECIALLY sex before marriage.

The worst part about being pregnant is that Angel was a married man who claimed that the reason he remained married was that he had a son who needed him to be there for him. His son was labeled as being "mentally retarded" because that was the term used in 1950. Confused and full of anxiety, Andrea broke the news to her aunt. Anger and frustration filled her aunt as she decided to take drastic measures to solve the issue. *"Voy a llamar a la policia"* ("I'm calling the police"). Terrified of the thought of Angel going to jail, Andrea told him to leave. So, he left.

Andrea moved out of her aunt's house, moved into a studio apartment, and started receiving welfare benefits. Again, her dream was placed on hold. As a single mother, Andrea began the struggle of raising a child by herself. It was not an easy task. One night, the baby continued to cry, and Andrea did not know what was wrong. She figured that the baby was spoiled and just wanted to be picked up, so she let her cry all night long.

That is really nothing to be proud of. This is the nurturing time when the warmth of a mother is substituted by the warmth of the womb. So it would have been okay to hold the baby. Well, that seemed to be a remedy for Andrea to deal with the baby's screaming. For seven months, Andrea struggled to support her baby until she could not handle it anymore and decided to take the baby to Puerto Rico to live with her parents while she worked and saved money. So she left her baby with her parents, sisters, and brother to temporarily care for her with the condition that once she became well established, she would return for her child.

Mr. Moneybags

Once back in New York, Andrea landed a job at a factory. Her aunt's husband introduced her to a friend of his; an older, not quite handsome, financially established, unmarried, baggage free, merchant marine who wanted to support her and her baby by offering marriage. "El es un buen proveedor" ("He is a good provider") "El es soltero, no como el otro" ("He is single, not like that other one"). Those were the words spoken to Andrea by her aunt about her husband's friend. There clearly was no interest on her behalf to learn about all the specifics pertaining to this man, as a matter of fact, she never mentioned his name. He was simply the man that her aunt wanted her to marry. "El te va a dar una buena vida" ("He will give you a good life.") She told Andrea this in her strict voice. All her troubles would end if she married this man. She was really not interested in him; but for the sake of getting her baby back, she was willing to accept him.

However, fate decreed that Angel would sneak back into Andrea's life. There was just something about that man that she couldn't resist. Then it happened again—she became pregnant again! With Angel still married and Andrea being a single mom with an unfulfilled dream, this pregnancy had to be terminated. History repeated itself and Angel fled. Unfortunately, he never got to meet his first child. Did he even make the effort to meet her? Had he ever been curious about the second pregnancy? There were a few times when Angel's sisters and Andrea would talk. That is how, not long after their last encounter; Andrea found out that while walking in an alley in Brooklyn, for reasons unknown, Angel was attacked. The news came like a flash, like a knife piercing through her heart. *"Alguien lo atacó"* ("Someone attacked him.") *"Le cortaron la cara!"* ("Someone cut his face!"), she was told.

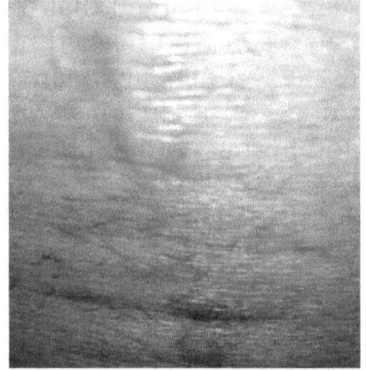

"Que quieres decir?" (*"What are you trying to say?"*). Andrea asked with her heart beating so hard that she thought it was coming out of her mouth. Though he survived, his face was sliced up, which caused him to have a huge scar beginning at the top of his cheek and ending down at his jawline. Andrea never got to see his scar or his face again. It was only a few years later that she found out that he was still married and living on Ludlow Street.

CHAPTER TWO

BACK ALLEY MIDWIFE

Desperation again reared its head in Andrea's mind. What was she going to do? She had no life or health insurance, no secured future, and no father for her babies, for she missed her opportunity with her uncle's friend to care for the first child, and then she let Angel slip away again after the second pregnancy. What to do? There *had* to be a way out! For five months, she hid her secret. Andrea was able to pull it off because the first time she got pregnant, she did not show until she was almost eight months pregnant; and this time was no different. Then, the thought entered her mind: Puerto Rico! Andrea could easily take care of the matter there. She went to her parents' house with the excuse that she was ready to bring her child back to New York. So she wrote a letter telling her parents that she was going back to Puerto Rico.

Andrea saved enough money to do what she needed to do. So, she bought a one-way ticket to her native land; once there, she would ask her family to buy her return ticket. Still keeping the secret from her aunt, she departed. Andrea's *mami* refused to let her take her child back, but there were no legal documents to prove that Andrea had given up her rights as a parent. So, there was the possibility that Andrea could win the argument. However, Andrea's *mami* was not concerned about legalities but with the fact that she believed that Andrea had left her child for her to raise. What followed was a series of arguments, finger pointing, regrets, and name calling. Andrea's *mami* was determined not to let the child go to an environment in which she felt the baby was not safe. After all, the child was loved and protected by all the members of the family. There was nothing any of them would not do to make sure the child was well taken care of. Andrea's *mami* was concerned because many things can happen when a parent is in a desperate situation.

After much fussing and arguing and discovering that Andrea was pregnant again, her *mami* won the battle to keep the child with her where she would be loved and well taken care of, which is what Andrea wanted in the first place. If Andrea returned to New York and got her life together, THEN she could go back and get her child.

Andrea's plan was coming together— her parents would continue to care for her child, and she would take care of the "other" matter. She had no money for a legal abortion, so her plan was to contact the neighborhood midwife, who could help her "take care of the matter." For just a few dollars, all Andrea had to do was to meet the midwife at her house.

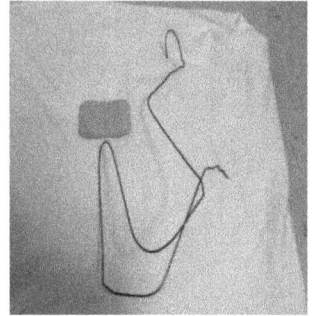

No doctors, no hospitals, no masks, no gloves, and no anesthesia were required. A bar of soap was used to "sanitize" the pubic area. To extract the fetus from the uterus, as barbaric as it sounds, a wire clothes hanger was inserted into the vagina. To make the procedure easier and less painful, Andrea had to drink castor oil, as nasty as it was, yet, it was probably better than feeling a lot of pain. That was what the midwife used to perform the "procedure." Would we call the midwife an abortionist? Would we call her an illegal doctor or nurse, a midwife with no license operating in filthy conditions, with no gloves, and no mask? Or could she be called a murderer?

In just a few moments, the fetus would no longer be a problem. As dangerous as this was, Andrea went for it. Well, dangerous it was indeed! Because of that procedure, she discovered later on that she could not have any more children. After the procedure, Andrea had no other choice than to delay her trip back to New York because she became ill. Feeling guilty for what she had done, she talked about it with her parents. Besides, where was she going to discard the fetus? In the trash can, at the beach, or in the river?

The male fetus' remains were buried in her parents' back yard. For him, there would be no hope of ever seeing the light of day; no hope of ever meeting his family; no hope of playing the games children play; no hope of learning of the birds and the bees; no hope of becoming someone; no hope of growing up with his sibling, and no hope of knowing what love could be. Andrea returned to New York where only her aunt knew about her recent actions.

THE WINDOW WATCHER (PART 2)

Back in New York, Andrea met Miguel; a widower, father of an adult daughter and son, a factory worker sixteen years her senior. Miguel was a leg man, so he immediately fell in love with Andrea after seeing her legs. Andrea made it clear that she was not in love with him and that if he wanted to get with her, he would have to marry her and send for her child. Miguel agreed, Andrea quit her job at the factory, and they married on a Thanksgiving Day. Soon afterward, they sent for the child. Miguel became the adoptive father. For years, the secret of Scarface, the real father, was swept under the rug.

While Andrea was the disciplinarian, Miguel was the lenient parent, not interfering in the child's upbringing except for providing for parochial school and all the childhood necessities. Miguel quit his job at the factory; and although he did not speak English well, he started working at a hospital in the kitchen as a butcher. There were hard times when Miguel got laid off and all there was to eat was white rice and fried eggs. Andrea had gained much weight over the years and by this time; she had been stricken with illness due to obesity. Weighing over 350 pounds, the doctor had no choice but to operate and remove her thyroids. The operation caused major psychological and physical problems. Andrea lost most of her hair; one leg swelled to the point that it never returned to normal; and her nerves became shattered. Andrea never endeavored to find a job outside the home. So Miguel carried the entire household financial load. Nonetheless, as stressful and devastating as those times were, Miguel did not lift a finger to hit his wife or his child.

Miguel had a routine that he followed. Basically, he was a family man who went from home to work and back home at the same time and ate at the same time. After dinner, he retired to the bedroom. On rare occasions, Miguel would buy pints of rum and would have a few shots, hang around in the living room, and get "happy," and that is when he became very talkative. Although it seemed apparent that Miguel was a working man who loved and provided for his family, he did get trapped in the net of his lustful desires and had an affair with one of the residents of their senior citizens' apartment complex. Learning of the affair caused Andrea and their daughter much heartache.

The Window Watcher, the one creeping into my room at night, the man gently rubbing my thighs was my **adoptive father**, Miguel. The scar-faced man, the one who fled twice from his responsibilities, was Angel, my **biological** father; the woman who gave up love to give her child a better life yet frequently beat her, was Manteco, mi *mami* **(my mother)**, Andrea; the Rolling Stone, the runaway in search of a better life; the womanizer in search of satisfying his sexual desires, the child molester who finally lay his head on the bed of that Puerto Rican river, was Juan, *mi abuelo* **(my grandfather)**, These are they who initially contributed to the bitterness and un-forgiveness that for years have weighed heavily in my heart, mind, and spirit.

HOT LIPS

This harassment or inappropriate behavior toward me as a little girl continued, this time, in the person of my adoptive father's brother, a heavy-set diabetic man who seemed enormous to me. For some reason, with beady eyes and an up-to-no-good gigantic smile, on one of his rare visit, he stood in our kitchen like he was waiting for something. Not suspecting anything, I entered and found myself in front of this man eying me up and down, then asking him if there was anything he needed there in the kitchen. No, he did not need anything; he just wanted "something." That something' was not in the kitchen; it was on my body—my virgin lips!

As he inched his way closer and closer to me, he spoke softly and told me how much I had grown up, how pretty I was. I did not find it unusual that he would say that I had grown-up or how pretty I was. This was common among family members and friends. I had heard that many times. It was when he got so close that his lips touched mine that I did not know how to react. Although my body felt as though it was frozen solid, here I stood with my eyes wide open, knees knocking, and hands shaking. I felt uncomfortable, yucky, and scared. No one had ever kissed me on the lips.

While struggling with the state of shock that I was in, images of another incident flashed across my mind. I was only eight years old the night that my *mami* was sent to the emergency room and a man acted inappropriately with me. I was entrusted to a neighbor who was hosting a party. That man, a guest, a nameless man, gently (there goes that gently again) drew me to his lap and took the can of beer that he was holding and brought it to my lips while someone else snapped a picture. Somehow, someone gave that picture to my *mami,* and I ended up keeping it. For years, I looked at that picture, not quite understanding what the man's purpose was in doing that.

What did I know? There was no harm in that. Did I even think there was any harm in that? I was an innocent child who did not know anything about the birds and the bees: had no clue. It was not until the moment in the kitchen with *tio Pablo* (Uncle *Pablo*) that I realized that what the man at the party was doing was wrong. In my mind's eye, he probably wanted to kiss me too or rub me against his lap. I felt uncomfortable with this flashback, just like I feel uncomfortable in the kitchen with *tio Pablo.*

Having *tio Pablo* kiss me on the lips was not a good feeling. My lips felt like hot sauce had been poured in my mouth. His manly lips were hot—not the hot that the young people use nowadays like cute hot, but literally burning hot! Of course, I left the kitchen as soon as I could. I did not say anything to anyone; but the approach, the sneakiness, the closeness, the burning of my little-girl lips became buried in my thoughts.

I still did not understand why this was happening and especially with someone who I believed to be a family member. All I know is that this man whom I called "tio Pablo" was supposed to be a role model, a family member who cared and should not do anything "bad" to little girls. This was unthinkable. Was this a pattern? Was this the way it was supposed to be? Not long after that incident, *tio* Pablo died and the secret of his inappropriate behavior died with him. Why didn't I say anything to anyone? I guess fright had a hold on me.

SISTER STICKY FINGERS (PART 1)

Somehow, I had irritated the nun, so she called me up in front of the class. I knew then that I was in for it. Parochial school was no joke! How did I end up there? I remember trying to get in line for assembly. I was lining up in front of a little girl named *Esperanza* (Hope). She didn't like me, and she didn't like the fact that I was standing in front of her. Out of anger, she took out her pencil and stabbed the area between my eyebrow and my eyelid. My fifth grade teacher, whose habit was to squeeze my cheeks (which by the way made me feel uncomfortable) told her to apologize to me. The incident caused my *mami* to transfer me out of the public school system and into parochial school.

I guess my smart mouth stems from my *mami's* strict upbringing. She insisted that I be an excellent student. The problem with that was that she had been very hard on me for as long as I could remember. Somehow I skipped kindergarten and moved on to the first grade, but I did not know my alphabet so she tried to teach it to me one day. I guess she expected me to learn it right away.

It was customary for my *mami* to take me to the movies to see Hispanic movies. So, on this particular day, an actress named Rosita Quintana starred in the movie "Cielito Lindo" (Pretty Sky). Anyway, IMMEDIATELY upon getting home from seeing the movie and with her stern voice she ordered: "Recita el abecedario" ("Recite the alphabet"). I couldn't remember it, or I didn't want to say all of the letters, so she took a small blackboard that she used to teach me at home, and she ordered me one more time—"Recita el abecedario" ("Recite the alphabet!") I still didn't recite all of it. So, she asked me another question. "Cual es el nombre de la actriz en la pelicula?" ("What is the name of the actress in the movie?") So I, with an "everybody knows that attitude," answered, "Rosita Quintana." Then, all of a sudden, out of nowhere, came what I least expected, WHAM!!! She took the blackboard and slammed it across my head, broke it, and ordered again, "AHORA, recita el abecedario" ("NOW, recite the alphabet!") So hysterically crying, I say "aaaaaaa (sob) bbbbbb (sob) cccccc" (sob). Never mind if I got a bump on my head, a contusion or a concussion. That, my friend, was the day I learned my ABCs.

So I guess I must have said something smart to the nun or maybe refused to answer a question because she called me up to the front of the class. With the ruler in one hand (this was no flimsy ruler either), and a piercing look in her eyes, then she told me to bend over. I knew when she said to bend over that my backside would end up (no pun intended) red and sore. I bent over and waited with anticipation with my head buried on the desktop as I peeked at my classmates—their heads turned toward me— one eye on the nun and the other on my bottom. I knew they were looking in fear and wonderment, for whacking one of us on the backside was a first for her. A few months earlier she had sent me to the bathroom to wash my mouth out for something I said, but she had done that to other children, but the whacking, that was a first! I had just recently experienced a similar situation where my bottom was going to be attacked. Did the nun want me to take down my little girl panties too? Why the ruler? Why the bending over? How hard was she going to hit me? I think the Lord sent some angels there to hold her hand because just as she was ready to strike, her arm was suspended in the air. I believe it was an angel that grabbed her arm and prevented her from slamming that ruler on my backside. For all of a sudden with twisted lips she quietly utters these words, "Go sit down." Huh? Was I happy? Heck yeah! Thinking things over, I probably could have told the parish priest (the pastor) or Mother Superior, I could have told my parents, but no, I didn't. I kept that incident in my mind and in my heart.

MRS. STICKY FINGERS

Here I go again, meeting up with another sticky finger. This time she was a fair skinned, red–haired, green-eyed Puerto Rican who was married to a tall, lanky-looking man. She was one of my *mami's* friends who lived in the same housing project. We lived on the eleventh floor, and she lived on the thirteenth. There was something strange about how the lady looked at me. Her eyes looked like cat eyes, and she looked like she drank alcohol regularly because her head shook a little when she talked, and her face looked red all the time. I remember one day, she stared at my face and told me that I have beautiful long lashes. It was the way she said it that was strange, but I went about my business and forgot about it until this particular day when my *mami* sent me to her apartment to pick up something—I cannot remember what. It was customary for me to run errands for my parents, so I did not find it strange to go there at my *mami's* request.

What was strange was the fact that as she handed me the object, she moved behind me, sort of slithering, like the snake in the *Garden of Eden*, and extended her right arm and reached for my chest. I felt my stomach turn. I froze. The next thing I knew was that she placed her whole arm underneath my blouse and in a circular motion; she rubbed the center of my left breast. This was a strange sensation; this lady's touch was painful. I do not remember how I broke loose; but I did, and grabbing the bag that she had for my *mami*, I dashed out the door and ran as fast as I could, even skipping some steps as I descended the hallway stairs.

My heart felt as though it was ready to explode right out of my chest. My chest—the same area this lady violated. My chest, a delicate area created to nourish a newborn baby. My chest was a private area that the woman had no business touching. As I reached the eleventh floor, I tried to catch my breath before knocking at our door. I knew my *mami* was going to notice, so I tried my best not to show my discomfort, disgust, and discontent. I was really embarrassed, so once again, I kept this mishandling of my body to myself.

CHAPTER THREE

. . . .

THE STOMPER

I did not see it coming—his size thirteen shoe striking down like lightning. He stepped on me like he was mashing grapes, preparing to make wine at a vineyard. He was so enraged that he probably did not fully realize that what he was mashing was a human being's ribs. Did he realize that with just that one heavy stomp he could kill me? Maybe he was so angry that he didn't care about rotting in prison?

Here I was lying on the living room floor, peering at the family's dumbfounded looks on all their faces as all eyes were upon me. Every breath I took made me feel as though my heart was ready to break through my skin. The more the family yelled at him to stop, the angrier he became and the harder he stomped. It took four persons to get him off me. I was in such excruciating pain that at first I did not notice that he had directed his anger towards a window—shattering it to pieces.

It was a miracle that my ribs were not bruised or broken. The pain was unbearable, I could hardly breathe, but I had to pretend there was nothing wrong because I had to face my parents.

This was not the first time this man hurt me. I remember the time when I found out that he was cheating on me with his first cousin. He became so angry that he pushed me down on top of the radiator and grabbed my neck and started choking me. Why did I put up with him? Why? Was love **that** blind? Was I suffering from low self-esteem? Did I think this was the only man in the world? Did I think he was better than me? I think the worst part of this entire ordeal was hiding it from my parents. It was hard to insert the key into the keyhole and open the door to my parents' apartment. I could hardly breathe. To speak felt like tons of bricks resting on my tongue. For weeks I endured the physical pain and humiliation from being stepped on like an unwanted bug. I never told my parents—I just couldn't.

MS. STICKY FINGERS

You would think that as an adult all the sexual harassment would have stopped, correct? Wrong! I was not eight anymore, nor eleven, and not even thirteen, but thirty-seven, YES, thirty-seven! I needed a break from New York, so much has happened living in the "hood" while raising my three sons alone. By this time, I had been divorced for nearly fourteen years, withdrawn from the City University of New York after two and half years, my *mami* had passed, my adoptive father's second wife had passed, and he had moved to Puerto Rico. Yes, all the childhood abuses had ended, but the memories still haunted me.

For the longest time, I had dreamt about leaving New York and moving to a more peaceful, less-congested town, somewhere, it really did not matter, just to get away was the idea. But, of course, living with limited resources, I kept dreaming but not really believing that it would be possible. Then, opportunity came knocking at my door. Yes! I had a chance to expand my horizons. I had a chance to go somewhere else in search for a better life. I knew a couple who had family in Virginia. They invited me to vacation with them; but with the proposal that if I liked it there, then I could move in with them for a while. I couldn't believe it. My job as an assistant teacher paid well, but I was searching for peace. So, I vacationed for two weeks in Virginia, but little did I know that I would fall in love with this beautiful place and decide to stay. I left New York with all of its drama and trauma. I knew that the images of the past would continue to haunt me; but at least, I would be in a better atmosphere that would eventually help with the healing process.

But, that process was soon interrupted the first month I arrived in my new home state. It did not take long for me to find an apartment; the problem was that the money that I had saved from my previous job would soon be history. Here I was in a place I knew nothing about. I did not drive; did not own a car; and I had not yet learned my way around. I found myself thinking that I was at the end of my rope. I looked up to the sky in desperation asking for a solution to this problem. I did *not* want to return to New York. I loved it here, and here is where I wanted to stay.

I did not have much in my apartment for all I brought with me was my six-and-a-half-year old child and luggage for a two weeks stay. I found myself amazed at this beautiful place where the backyard was spacious enough for my son to play and where I did not have to worry about him getting run over by a car. I set out to explore this huge yard, and I found that on the other side were individual houses. So, I walked across it, and that is when I met two women. We immediately connected. I started telling my story about how and why I was in Virginia, and the fact that I desperately needed a job. Fascinated by my story and enjoying the sound of my voice (she liked my accent), one of the ladies offered to take me to her two jobs so that I might work. One of the jobs was cleaning offices at a car dealership, and the other was as a housekeeper at a well-known hotel—both in Newport News, Virginia.

What did I know about cleaning offices and cleaning hotel rooms? My education was in early childhood development and so was my work experience. Nonetheless, I was excited about making a living for my child and me. This meant I could stay in Virginia. I have always been a quick learner; plus, the woman showed me some tricks to cleaning without hurting my back or taking too much time on one room.

In three months' time, we became very close, too close, I might say, because we were back and forth in each other's houses. I was at her house more than she was at my apartment. By working two jobs, there really was not much time for socializing. On one particular night, I went over and that is when she asked me if I had ever been kissed by a woman. But as she asked, she inched closer and closer to me, pushed me onto her bed, and while lying on top of me, "I froze". All of a sudden her lower body started grinding on my lower body parts. Again, like years earlier, somehow I broke loose and went home confused and worried.

Not knowing what would happen in the morning, I got ready for work and waited. I was not sure what I was going to say or what she would say, so I just waited. I waited and waited. I saw the time was drawing closer to the time to leave for work, so I called her, but she didn't answer. On that day I missed out on work for she had left without me. That evening, I went to her house and her son let me in, and I asked her why she did not pick me up. Her response was that she did not *have* to take me anywhere. Well, I lost both my jobs. Not long after, I found out that she had a heart attack and died, leaving a fourteen-year-old son with no one to raise him. She died and so did the incidents.

The years of the sexual and physical abuse that I endured as a child, pre-teen, a teenager, and even as an adult had ended with her death.

REFLECTIONS

I endured many years of sexual and physical abuse. It has been very difficult to erase those past images from my mind—images that are embedded, not only in my mind but in my spirit and in my heart. Nightmare after nightmare has filled my subconscious mind. Nerve-racking sweats have filled my pillows as I tossed and turned on my bed every night in hopes of finding a comfortable position that would block those images and make them disappear.

But, the images did not fade away. They kept lingering on and on, over and over again. Throughout the years, I've heard stories of women who have been raped, sexually molested, physically beaten, and emotionally harassed to the point that they traded their God-given self-esteem for the low self-esteem that had been imposed on them by their abusers. Because of harassment, maybe some of them or probably all of them have overlooked their God-given self-esteem and substituted it for bitterness and an unforgiving heart. Bitterness and an unforgiving heart may have caused them to bury their devastating experiences into their memory banks. I was no different. I just wanted to get even.

For years, I struggled with the fact that my *mami* left me (an infant) crying all night long. What was so hard about holding me? Maybe I did not need to be fed. Maybe I did not need a diaper change. Maybe I did not need to be burped. All I needed was to just feel the warmth of her embrace. I believe that was the main reason for my abandonment issues. I had trouble saying good-bye. It was hard to part with any family member visiting from Puerto Rico. I was a royal mess from the moment I stepped into the airport until the airplane took off. I carried that issue even as an adult. In 2001, my pastor was assigned to another church in another city, and I believe that I cried the loudest and the longest.

Not only did I struggle with the fact that my *mami* left me crying all night long, but I also struggled with the fact that I could have had a maternal brother, nieces, and nephews had she not had that abortion. I have a maternal brother (of my birthed father), perhaps nieces, and nephews; but I never met them. I say never, because at this stage in life, I gave up the idea of trying to find any of them. I would not know where to begin because I do not know if my biological father is still alive. On June 2, 2014, my mami my would have been eighty-six years, seven months and two days old. So, there is no telling how old he is or would have been.

I could not accept my *mami's* decision to abort my brother. I did not understand the hardship that she had gone through. The bitterness in my heart was more than logic or explanations could explain. It was all about how I felt, how I could not play with my brother, how she should have just had the baby and left him with my grandparents, then come back for us. I grew up an only child. My nine cousins who lived in the tenement apartment above us were like my brothers and sisters.

Beginning at the age of seven—yes—seven, I baby-sat my nine cousins. One of my aunts had two sets of twins. We lived in the same tenement apartments until my parents and I moved to the projects. Although we moved, we would still visit, and what was great was that we were just twelve blocks and one avenue away. While they were still at the apartment, the older ones, and I practically did everything together. We stepped on roaches together. We jumped on top of the bed whenever we saw a mouse together. We played all the outdoor-and-indoor games together.

We not only played together—we cried together. I remember the day the oldest of the nine fell down the stairs holding a pencil in one hand. The result of that fall was horrific. The pencil stabbed his head and there was blood all over the place. It did not take long for the ambulance to get there. Seeing my cousin at the end of the stairs, with his head drenched in blood, reminded me of the previous month when one of the neighborhood teens shot himself in the head. In my mind was the image of seeing him in that cold casket in the middle of his *mami's* living room and folks crying over the body. His head was covered with a man's white handkerchief so that no one would see the hole in his head. Yes, I was there; it was my first of many funerals. As gruesome as that sight was, it was nothing compared to that day when I experienced that ghastly impressionable moment when my cousin fell. I was petrified that he might end up in a cold casket like that other unfortunate young man.

After my parents and I moved to the projects, we were playing outside, and one of the neighborhood children started picking on him, so I ran over to the benches where all the mothers were sitting, gossiping of course, and I told on the boy. Well, one of the other *mamis*, Ana *la Dominicana*, was highly upset. The other women named her Ana *la Dominicana* because she was the only Dominican there amongst the *rest of the Puerto Rican women. The women identified* her, yes, by her first name—Anna, but also by her nationality. Why? I do not know; I was only ten years old. Whatever the grown folks said, we young ones repeated, no questions asked. Anyway, when I went over to tell one of the mothers that her son was picking on my cousin, Anna *la Dominicana* told my *mami* that I was a "picapleitos" (an instigator) (a fight provoker).I really did not understand why she called me that because a *picapleitos* is considered to be a litigious lawyer. I think she wanted to call me a snitch or a tattletale. The next thing we saw was our neighborhood *mami's* screaming at the top of their lungs all manner of stuff that should not have spewed out of their mouths. While it is true that they would beat the living daylights out of us, they still did not like the idea of other women putting their children down. No, in this case it did not take a village to raise a child.

Yes, we went through a lot at such young ages. Whenever there was a fire where they lived, my parents would provide shelter for the ones in need. The girls would sleep with me in my room, and the boys would sleep on pillows and blankets on the living room floor. They were my first cousins whom I considered to be the brothers and sisters that I had, but never met. Although, time and distance have kept us apart all these years, I still hold them close to my heart. When we don't communicate by phone or Facebook, they are in my thoughts and prayers.

Not only was I bothered by the fact that my mami sent my biological father away, I was left crying all night long, and my brother was never born. I was also bothered by the unjust beatings that I was subjected to by the hands of my *mami*, sometimes with an extension cord, other times with a belt and still others times with her stern hands. Finally, I was bothered by the fact that I suspected her suspicion of my father's sexual molestation and attempts of rape and kept it quiet. This I sensed because not long before she passed, she started to ask me the dreaded question. I remember her words, "quiero preguntarte algo" (I want to ask you something but we were interrupted. I can't remember what it was, but I think my father came in. I knew in my heart that she was going to ask me if he had ever tried to molest me. It stands to reason that she might have felt the absence of his presence in her bed and wondered why he would be up for so long in the middle of the night. Perhaps, if she would have called him and acknowledged that she knew something was going on, then perhaps things would have been different. I might have had a softer spot for her in my heart.

But, I think she was afraid deep down inside because she must have felt trapped. Her dreams were not all fulfilled. She never went back to work; and when she tried to make some money babysitting, it was I who ended up watching the children. I think she was afraid that she would not survive without her husband.

For years, I took care of my *mami* when she became ill. I was managing two households from the age of eighteen until the age of thirty-three. She basically became a recluse. Her social life consisted of watching Spanish soap operas, game shows, and playing the street numbers. Of course, I had to make the runs for her. It was hard for me to shop for her since she was very particular. My likes were not the same as hers. It was hard shopping for her clothes because after her thyroid operation, she had gained over 300 pounds, and there were only two stores noted for selling plus size clothing. Back then they were not called plus sizes, just by the numbers 2X, 3X, 4X, 50, 54, 56, and 60.

It was also difficult buying shoes for her, because her right instep had a lump that only allowed her to wear a low-cut shoe. She had to wear triple XXX; and of course, they were almost as expensive as the clothes. Since she did not leave her apartment, I think the most disappointing part was searching store to store, bringing back a pair of shoes, and then having to go back to the store to return them because they would not fit that right foot. Although she had stopped going out, she still wanted shoes because she loved shoes. I remember her playing that number 876, her favorite, because according to her, it was interpreted as the number for dreaming about shoes. So figure! To each his/her own!

For a while, I thought that taking care of my *mami* caused my marriage to suffer because I was called a momma's girl and many of the marital arguments centered on the fact that I ran both households. I figured that since I was doing such an excellent job taking care of both households, and since my mami did not have any other children, I was doing what I was supposed to do. The last thing that I expected was to be called a momma's girl. I was an only child and not until my father retired did the load minimize. My husband had vowed to love me in all circumstances; I thought that included helping out our parents; especially if they became sick or disabled. I guess I wasn't loved enough for him to be able to understand that it was necessary for me to do what I did. No, I was not a momma's girl. I had learned to be independent at an early age. I had learned to cook, clean, iron, shop, budget, and baby-sit.

Whenever my *mami* needed me, there I was. I dropped out of school while in my junior year in high school to take care of her. By the age of thirty-three, I had been married, gone through a nasty divorce, given birth to three sons, completed clerical classes at Manpower, worked full time and *still* managed to care for my *mami*. When my father retired, he was able to help out more in their household. When my *mami* became very ill, she requested to die at home, since dying in a hospital was out of the question. I had honored her request not to be hospitalized. She passed away peacefully on her bed less than two weeks after Mothers' Day. I was in charge of all the funeral and burial arrangements. Yes, in spite of all the pain and burden of the past, in spite of all the blood, sweat, and tears, and in spite of how I felt about my *mami* and her treatment towards me; I was still there until the day that she died. Isn't that what a daughter is supposed to do?

No, I did not take care of my grandfather, the midwife, my biological father, my adoptive father, *Tio Pablo*, my *mami's* neighbor, my neighbor, the nun, and the long-lost love like I did my *mami*. I just kept things quiet like a scared little bunny. Some of these people I had never met, yet, they left a bitter impact on my life. Although, I resented their actions towards me; and of course, deep down in my inner being I would think of telling on them and to get even, nothing that I could ever do to any one of these people could compare to what God can do. God's wrath is billions of times worse than mine could ever be.

I did not know this at that time, but this specific commandment, found in the New Testament, has helped me overcome un-forgiveness.

> *"Do not repay evil for evil or abuse for abuse; but, on the contrary, repay with a blessing. It is for this that you were called—that you might inherit a blessing. For those who desire life and desire to see good days, let them keep their tongues from evil and their lips from speaking deceit; let them turn away from evil and do good; let them seek peace and pursue it. For the eyes of the Lord are on the righteous, and his ears are open to their prayer. But the face of the Lord is against those who do evil."* (1 Peter 3:9-12) (NRSV).

Not only did I learn from that Scripture it helped me with my unforgiving issues, but I also discovered a life-changing characteristic of God found in the Old Testament that has kept me on the straight and narrow path.

"There are six things that the Lord hates, seven that are an abomination to him: haughty eyes, a lying tongue, and hands that shed innocent blood, a heart that devises wicked plans, feet that hurry to run to evil, a lying witness who testifies falsely, and one who sows discord in a family" (Proverbs 6:16-19) (NRSV).

And, throughout my journey here on earth from the one with haughty eyes to the one who sows discord in a family, folks with those characteristics and ungodly acts have crossed my path; however, it is not up to me to judge or condemn. I learned that vengeance is not mine, and that I serve a God who loves me enough to invent instructions that guide me into a righteous life and help me to understand that everyone has a chance at redemption and that I am in His plan to assist others in the process, even those who have abused me.

"My friends, if anyone is detected in a transgression, you who have received the Spirit should restore such a one in a spirit of gentleness. Take care that you yourselves are not tempted" (Galatians 6:1-18) (NRSV).

TAMAR

Physical and sexual abuses are not recent inappropriate human behaviors. You can go back as far as Biblical times. I read about one young lady named Tamar. Tamar was Absalom's (King David's son's) virgin sister; a beautiful young woman indeed, according to the writer of 2 Samuel. David's other son, Amnon; fell in love with his sister. Amnon did not look upon his sister with brotherly eyes but with lust. Since a boyfriend and girlfriend or husband and wife relationship was out of the question, Ammon became so tormented that he made himself sick. Amnon felt he had to find a way to get intimate with Tamar.

Jonadab, a friend of Amnon, who was a slick guy, was concerned about his health and asked him what was going on. Amnon told him that he loved his brother Absalom's sister, instead of saying he loved his own sister. Jonadab's suggestion was for Amnon to trick his sister into going to bed with him by asking David to have Tamar cook for him because he was ill. Amnon convinced David to send Tamar so that she could cook in front of him so that he could eat from her hand while in bed.

Amnon's wish came true because Tamar made cakes in front of him. After Tamar went through all that trouble, Amnon refused to eat. He threw everyone out of the room, except for Tamar, whom he grabbed and forced into bed with him. Tamar refused to lie with him, but Amnon didn't care; he had his way with her, and afterward, he threw her out too, despising her with all his being.

To Tamar, the act of rejection and throwing her out was more hurtful than the despicable act of rape. Tamar was thrown out of the room, and the door was bolted behind her. She puts ashes on her head and rips her long robe; then, she puts her hand on her head and cries loudly and leaves the room. Tamar ran into her brother Absalom, who asks her if Amnon had forced her. Absalom told Tamar to keep quiet about the rape because Amnon was her brother. He even told her to not worry about what had happened to her. Tamar went to live with her brother Absalom and became a lonely woman. Then, Amnon met his fate by the hands of Absalom, who had him killed in an act of revenge for what he did to his sister.

FROM ME TO TAMAR

Tamar, it was not your fault and it was not fair that you spent the rest of your life ashamed and lonely because of someone else imposing his lustful desires on you *"for all that is in the world—the desire of the flesh, the desire of the eyes, the pride in riches—comes not from the Father but from the world"* (1st John 2:16) (NRSV).

> *"Do you not know that you are God's temple and that God's Spirit dwells in you? If anyone destroys God's temple, God will destroy that person. "For God's temple is holy, and you are that temple"* (1 Corinthians 3:16-17) (NRSV).

> *"Therefore take up the whole armor of God, so that you may be able to withstand on that evil day, and having done everything, to stand firm. Stand therefore, and fasten the belt of truth around your waist, and put on the breastplate of righteousness. As shoes for your feet put on whatever will make you ready to proclaim the gospel of peace. With all of these, take the shield of faith, with which you will be able to quench all the flaming arrows of the evil one. Take the helmet of salvation, and the sword of the Spirit, which is the word of God"* (Ephesians 6:13-17) (NRSV).

"(For) *Indeed, the word of God is living and active, sharper than any two-edged sword, piercing until it divides soul from spirit, joints from marrow; it is able to judge the thoughts and intentions of the heart. And before him no creature is hidden, but all are naked and laid bare to the eyes of the one to whom we must render an account"* (Hebrews 4:12-16) (NRSV).

And my dear friend, remember this, "*The Lord is your keeper; the Lord is your shade at your right hand. The sun shall not strike you by day, nor the moon by night. The Lord will keep you from all evil; he will keep your life. The Lord will keep your going out and your coming in from this time on and forevermore*" (Psalm 121:5-8) (NRSV).

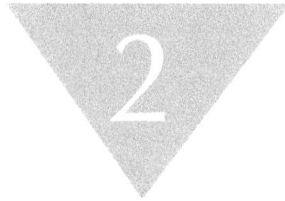

2

SECTION
TWO

Emotional and Spiritual Abuse

CHAPTER FOUR

. . . .

REFLECTIONS

Healing from sexual and physical abuse is difficult enough without having to worry about emotional and spiritual abuse. It just seems like the plot gets thicker and thicker, doesn't it? Emotional abuse encompasses many areas. How do I pinpoint emotional abuse other than to relate to whom and how he or she contributed to my personal conclusion—what I felt and who made me feel the way I felt; I call it abuse? Did I know I was being emotionally abused? No, I just thought that was the way it was supposed to be: adults yelling or saying things to us to correct us. Little did I know that what they were doing was detrimental to our health; it just felt bad and made me feel that most of what I was doing was wrong. I felt as though I was not capable of doing better.

The pain of emotional abuse was felt in my heart but affected my mind and the way I felt about myself. The scars left from emotional abuse are not physically visible to others and to me, but they invisibly pierced my heart and caused me to be on guard and careful about whom to trust. Name-calling is a form of emotional abuse. The constant defining of someone by something or someone other than what the person is or because of what the person does is to me a form of emotional abuse. It bothered me when grown folks called little children "monsters," "imps," "brats," or even when the younger generation uses the dreaded "n" word to identify each other.

"The mouth of the righteous is a fountain of life, but the mouth of the wicked conceals violence" (Proverbs 10:11) (NRSV).

THE HEAD SLAPPER

Here I am seven years old, yes, seven! That is as far as I can remember being in the kitchen and cooking something. I do not receive instructions on how to brew the *café* (coffee). You see, in my culture, we use ground coffee. It is scooped into a saucepan filled with boiled water, then poured into a colander. The brand *Bustelo* is the preferred one. I was not told how much *café* or water to use; so I poured the entire bag (one pound) of the ground coffee beans into a medium-sized saucepan. All of a sudden one of my relatives, who shall remain nameless, R.I.P., comes in yelling at the top of her lungs, "Are you Greek?" That's her favorite saying because according to her, Greek is a language that Puerto Ricans do not speak, read, or understand. So she slaps me across the head and yells *"Eres Griega?* ("Are you Greek"?)

I felt hurt and embarrassed. Though this is the same way that she responded to her own children, and I should be happy she considered me like one of her children. The name calling and slapping on the head put a damper on my emotions. It hurt my little girl feelings. This is a behavior that is hard to forget; but yet, since I understand that this was her way of dealing with things, I learned to accept it.

I think one of the reasons why I accepted this type of treatment was because my *mami* was no different. One of the phrases that has remained with me throughout the years is *"tu nunca te fijas"* ("you never focus"), which is to say that I never pay attention; or in other words, I interpreted that to mean that I am a scatterbrain. For years, I believed that she had placed a curse on me because I kept losing and misplacing things. Every single time that happened, the same poison would spew out of her mouth *"tu nunca te fijas"*. And so every time I hear the word *Greek*, I associate it with a slap on the head; and every time I misplace something, I relate it to my *mami's* negative words.

There were so many things my *mami* said to me that were hurtful and left a negative impact in my life, but one of the most hurtful things she did to me was the day I baked a cake, and it fell flat. She yelled at me in such an ugly manner that for years, I did not bake cakes. It shattered my self-esteem, and it destroyed my confidence in baking. I had a right to be bitter and resentful because negative words hurt. Words are detrimental to one's emotional and mental state of being, especially at a tender age.

Sister Sticky Fingers (Part 2

While struggling with the feelings of confusion, fear and distrust of being sexually molested and still dealing with the embarrassment of being called to the front of the class and almost getting my bottom hit with a ruler; once again, I was humiliated in front of the class. I remember correcting the nun for something; I cannot even remember what for, but she became so upset with me that she grounded me from going with the class to see "The Sound of Music." For years, every time I heard "the hills are alive with the sound of music," I cringed. I couldn't stand it. But, of course, time has helped me with the healing of my wounds.

I still have not seen the movie, but I no longer cringe. That was over fifty years ago, and yes, I don't forget, but I have forgiven. God showed me that no matter how right one might be, a person in authority with an inflated ego will try anything to bring you down and overpower you. I call it being on a power trip.

The Tattletale

Five years passed since "The Sound of Music" and the images of my grandfather and the other abusive folks and their behaviors remained vividly in my mind; and now to add to the bitterness, fate had it that what I had believed approximately for thirteen years; it had now come to a close. I lived with the notion that Miguel was my biological father. For that reason, I did not tell my mami about the times that he sneaked into my room at night. It had been a few years since he stopped, but the memories still lingered on. And every single night I lie down in bed with one eye open, scared that he might start sneaking in again, especially since I was now a fully developed woman engaged to be married. If you think you are reading wrong, well, no, I was seventeen years and nine months old when I married the first time. Besides thinking that I was in love, it was the opportunity to officially leave my parents' home.

So, here I was in the midst of all the wedding preparations when, to my surprise, a family member approached me. I do not know what came over her. I am not sure if there had been some lingering family issues and this person wanted to get even with my mami, but she pulled me aside and revealed the secret that had been kept for so many years, "Miguel is not your father!" How did this make me feel?

I felt flabbergasted, confused, and so angry that I wanted to scream. Hearing this contributed to my bitterness. I could not seem to shake off this feeling.

Who was I angry with? Was I angry with my mami for not telling me or for letting my real father get away? Was I angry at this person for knowing all these years and not telling me? Was I angry because I could have told on this man and didn't? Was I angry because not only was I told that I had a biological father somewhere, but also that I had a brother with Down syndromes, and heaven knows how many other brothers and sisters.

The straw that broke the camel's back was not when I was told that I could possibly have more than one brother and who knows how many sisters, but that my mami illegally aborted a fetus that could have been born to be my brother to grow up with me, cry with me, play with me, and could have been getting ready to see me walk down the aisle on my wedding day. I felt as though I was being robbed of that experience. The funny thing was that I kept my pain to myself, and this added to that lingering bitterness.

THE LONG-LOST BFF

Well, I did get married, but my marriage lasted less than three years. I was heartbroken because it was not a decision that I made. Here I am at the age of nineteen getting ready to become a divorcée with two children. It was at this time that I needed a comforting shoulder to cry on. Where else besides your family do you expect to receive support and encouragement? The tender voice of one saying "I'm here for you" or "I've got your back"? This is what I expect from my BFF.

I have known my BFF since the age of ten. Like some of the kids in the neighborhood, we cut our fingers, bleed a little, and press together and swear that we will be friends forever and ever. We jumped rope and played Jacks and Hula Hoop together. My BFF hands me down her clothes. To visit my BFF, I have to first ask permission, and that cannot be during dinner because her mom does not let me in. Her dad and brothers are different from her mom. Her brothers are nice looking, clean cut, and well-mannered young fellows. Her dad was or still might be a kind, soft-spoken, wholesome looking Christian man from the Pentecostal denomination. I remember visiting his church one day and the members were screaming and running up and down the aisles. I did not understand it at that time, and it freaked me out. I never went back to that particular church.

So, here I am, twelve years later, being divorced unfairly and against my will, heartbroken, and feeling abandoned and in need of comfort and encouragement, and I expected my BFF, the one I have shared secrets with, to be there for me. Instead, she abandoned me. She disappeared out of my life without an explanation. For years, I thought about her and wondered why. Wondering has become an obsession for me. For nearly forty years, I remembered her birthday (the same month as mine). For nearly forty years, I've wondered if she had ever thought about me or how her absence has affected me. It has been nearly forty years of being bitter and feeling drowned by the memories of our childhood and young adult years—nearly forty years waiting for closure. Well, my friends, those days are over. The Bible tells me that *those who withhold kindness from a friend forsake the fear of the Almighty* (Job 6:14) (NRSV). So why should I agonize and place so much importance on being forsaken if there are those who have forsaken more important things than me, like the fear of God? And to make me feel even better, Proverbs 25:19 tells me that to have trust in an unfaithful person is like having a bad tooth or lame foot; and I can't stand toothaches. So, to ultimately conquer the past pain and bitterness of a long-lost BFF, I did as Colossians 3:12-13 says, that as one of God's chosen ones, holy and beloved, I need to clothe myself with compassion, kindness, humility, meekness, and patience. I need to bear with others and if I have a complaint against another, I need to forgive just like the Lord has forgiven me.

I must forgive; she is not necessary for me to keep on living. She was not/is not the air that I breathe or the bread that sustains me or the water that quenches my thirst. An explanation or an apology is no longer necessary. Believe it or not as I write this portion of my memoir, I reflect on yesteryear's long-term search for this woman. I was listening to *Jeopardy,* and I heard one contestant's name that sounded like the long-lost BFF's ex-husband's name and I decided to search on Facebook to see if he had an account. Lo and behold, there he was! So, I messaged him, asking him if he knew the whereabouts of his ex-wife. But, he did not respond, so being myself, I had to take it a step further and check things out for myself. And again, lo and behold, there she was on Facebook, all smiles and looking like she was living a good life. Her mom had passed, but her dad and brothers were still alive. SMH (shaking my head) I did not know how to react except for "hmm hmm hmm, I don't believe it!"

THE MONEY GRABBER

It felt strange moving back in with my parents. But, I had no other choice because I had two boys to support and for a struggling divorcee, my parents' apartment was the most economically feasible place to stay. Back in my own room, this time with my two sons, so I did not think that there would be any "window watching." In an attempt to better myself, I took clerical classes at Manpower in Manhattan. I gave the fifty dollars that they paid me to my parents to cover the cost of my staying in my room. I was still under their control because my phone calls and going out were monitored. But, I dealt with it because I knew that soon I would be on my own. After all, I *was* twenty-two (22) years old, divorced, and a mother of two.

It was during this time that I noticed that Miguel's son and daughter stopped coming around. His son was now married. But there was something about his wife that I could not quite grasp. The next thing I knew, he no longer visited and neither did his sister. My father did stay in contact with them. Even though they were grown, he still gave them money from his Social Security check. That did not bother me. He gave me money too; and even if he didn't, it would not bother me. I too was his child; after all, I legally carried his last name. Although my boys carried their father's name, my father cared for them as though they were his flesh and blood grandchildren. To them, my father was their grandfather. Miguel became so attached to my two sons that he promised to leave them an inheritance.

However, fate had it—those years after my *mami* passed, and Miguel's second wife passed that he moved to Puerto Rico. We remained in contact via telephone until one day, the calls stopped coming in. Wondering what was going on, I called him, but the number was disconnected. The next thing to do was to call his neighbor. I had spoken with him several times, so I knew he didn't mind my calling. To my surprise, the neighbor was astonished when he heard my voice. He asked that dreaded question very common in my culture, *"Usted no sabia?"* (You didn't know?). Although my heart was pounding because I suspected the worst, I still asked the question *"Sabia que?"* (Know what?) *"Su papá se murió"* (Your father has died.), he told me. I think all of my ancestry mixtures (French, Taíno, African, Puerto Rican, and who knew what else) started rising up inside of me and holding the phone as tightly as I could, in anger I asked, "Why wasn't I informed?" The neighbor explained that when he called Miguel's daughter, he thought she was me but was shocked because I had not shown him respect. I appreciated him because he had been watching over my father. How could this be the same woman? But he thought she was me because Miguel failed to mention that he had two daughters.

According to the neighbor, the daughter whom he thought was me went to Puerto Rico and insulted him because he buried my father too quickly. It was my father's wish to be buried immediately upon his death. There was no viewing of the body or wake, so the neighbor, being also his friend, honored his last wishes. Besides insulting the neighbor, the daughter threw away all of my father's personal belongings, including pictures of my *mami*, my sons, and me. I guess she did not have any use for them. On his dresser he kept a picture of my oldest son at six years old. Why not? After all, they were very close and my son did consider him to be his grandfather. He even named him Tava. No one knew how he came up with it. You would think that he would call him *"abuelo"* or *"abuelito."* Tava is not Spanish. Years later, I discovered that Tava meant some sort of frying pan. How appropriate for a man who worked as a butcher!

According to the neighbor, the daughter had been there recently, at which time my father withdrew $25,000 from the bank and gave it to her. The paperwork where it was written that my sons and I would get some money was nowhere to be found. I felt slighted. I had been denied the opportunity to grieve at the time of his death. Of course I wanted some answers. Even though we had not been in contact, in heaven knows how many years, and I did not know her number nor did I know her last name, so I looked it up. Viola! I found her number. I called her and granted her the chance to explain her version of the events. She was very hostile towards me and threw it in my face that she was the only legitimate daughter. Of course, my feelings were hurt.

For years I had been the one running back and forth between households helping Miguel when my mami became ill. Every time he got laid off from work, his other daughter was nowhere to be found. Whenever he was sick, she was nowhere to be found. Yes, the memory of this man's inappropriate intentions towards me as a little girl remained in my memory, but so did his acts of kindness when he married my mother, gave me a name, supported me, and cared for my sons as though they were his own flesh and blood.

The entire focus was not on what my adoptive father wanted to do to me, but on how I survived the pain to overcome that childhood bitterness by seeing him through God's eyes. Also, how I was able to understand that although the flesh is weak, we are not born intentionally desiring to hurt someone but are capable of doing so. There are choices we make; there are entities in the atmosphere that provoke and tempt us. So yes, I did shed some tears when I found out he had passed. I did think of the good that he had done throughout the years. He had provided for and protected my mami and me. It pained me to know that the promise my adoptive father made to my sons would never come to pass. The money in my father's bank account was frozen. According to the bank manager, the only way to access my father's account was by his three offspring going to Puerto Rico and producing birth certificates. That meant my "brother," "sister," and me. That would never be possible because my brother had never responded to the letter I sent him, and my sister, well, you know the story.

Our conversation ended on a sour note. She was just another person to add to my list of persons who had hurt me in the past. I named her the Money Grabber because that is all she had done throughout the years; just grabbed my father's money. Even though my feelings were hurt, life went on. I did not need her to survive because in Ephesians 1:11, I am assured that I have been predestined by my heavenly Father to gain an inheritance. That inheritance is not of this world. Yes, we do need money to survive in this physical world, but we also need love and strong relationships. I did not know what his daughter was going through, and what caused that urgency to go get the money before his death, but I do know that if she would not have distanced herself from me, with God's intervention, we could have worked something out. That episode in my life was the straw that broke the camel's back. That was the last time I cried bitter tears over something that someone said or did to me to cause me emotional pain. My reaction toward emotional abuse is different now.

Yes, as a saved child of God, I am a target for the enemy; I just have to stay prayed up and understand that this Christian journey is no joke. I have been emotionally injured many times, but the incidents mentioned here are the most pressing because they involved family and close relationships, yet, I forgave them and moved on.

CHAPTER FIVE

SPIRITUAL ABUSE

. . . .

THE BACKSLIDER

Discovering that my father had passed after he was buried and reflecting on the conversation with his daughter centering on money was certainly emotionally draining, yet those feelings certainly did not hinder my praise. I praised God for not being controlled by the love of money. *For the love of money is a root of all kinds of evil, and in their eagerness to be rich some have wandered away from the faith and pierced themselves with many pains* (1 Timothy 6:10). Well, I certainly did not want to wander away from my faith. I still don't what to wander from my faith in God. It is my faith that keeps me strong enough to bear the pain of the past. It was my faith that helped me to move forward and to "*Press on toward to the goal for the prize of the heavenly call of God in Christ Jesus"* (Philippians 3:14) (NRSV).

In order to press forward, I had to leave behind all the bitterness that the past had brought me; this was easier said than done. Not only did I have to leave behind the pain of being abused sexually, physically, and emotionally but also spiritually as an adult. I say as an adult because I didn't get to truly understand my spirituality until the age of forty-four. Yes, church was a major part of my upbringing. Baptism, Confession, Holy Communion, Confirmation, and Holy Matrimony were the "sacraments" that I had partaken as part of my previous belief. I no longer recognize Confession, Confirmation, Holy Matrimony or Holy Orders and Extreme Unction as sacraments, only

Baptism and Holy Communion. However, my salvation does not come from Baptism or Holy Communion. I said it once, and I kept saying it again and again that I surely thought I was going to hell because I thought being good was the only way to get to heaven, and certainly, I was never good enough to earn that right. Going to church with my *mami* was a hair-raising experience. If I moved around too much, I got "the look." Oh, my word! "The look" was enough to make me cry. If I started to giggle, (and that I did a lot of) I got elbowed. Being confirmed was a trip. Just picture it: the Mass was in Latin; and when it was my turn to go up to the altar, the Bishop said *"Pateco"* (I think it means "peace to you.") Of course, I could not help but laugh and laugh. I laughed so hard that my face turned purple. Not only did the bishop slap me—my *mami* took hold of me too by pinching me as hard as she could. I think that was the last time I laughed in church by making fun of something so sacred.

Since the age of ten, through religious instruction (the Catechism), my understanding of faith has been that God is everywhere and that there are three persons in one God—the Father, Son, and Holy Ghost. God is to be feared, and Jesus Christ is his only begotten Son. I believed in the Holy Trinity. Yes, I believed in the Apostles' Creed. Yes, I believed that Jesus was born of the Virgin Mary. Yes, that is what I was taught but did not believe she remained a virgin. Surprise! Yes, that was the extent of my spirituality until the age of 22 when awareness came over me that what I had believed was told to me and not what I had discovered for myself. So, here I am at the age of 22, shifting away from the church. Many folks call that "backsliding." I started questioning the rituals that this particular denomination embraced. And just as the "whys" frequently kept popping in and out of my mind, so did I pop in and out of church. Nonetheless, I followed my family's tradition and had my children baptized and participate in their first Holy Communion. I had no problem with baptism or communion; it was the confessing to a clergyman, doing the sign of the cross every time I passed a church, getting slapped by a clergyman to confirm my faith, and reciting a myriad of Hail Mary's and Our Fathers as a sign of repentance, and the exclusion of women preachers, that rubbed me the wrong way. In search for clarification, I finally left that denomination.

On August 23, 1988, I left New York City to vacation in Virginia for two weeks, and twenty five years later, here I am. It takes seven more years before I find what I was looking for. Within two weeks, I found an apartment and a steady job. Through an associate, I meet her brother, my future husband. And not only did I meet her brother, I also met her mother, my future mother-in-law (R.I.P.). As a matter of fact, they both conspired to unite Arthur and me. Well, they succeeded, and Arthur and I got married in 1991.

Ah, my mother-in-law! She was a Jesus-loving, Holy Ghost-filled churchgoing woman of God who started taking my eight-year old son to church as soon as Art and I started dating. Of course, I did not go because the "whys" continued to pop in and out of my head. However, fate had it that my son was cast in a Christmas play immediately after a church service; and since I loved my child, I went to the service and stayed for the play. And then it happened! The sermon! Oh wow! I had never heard a sermon before. It seemed as though this pastor was preaching about my past life. I had been accustomed to listening to homilies, but this was different. This was personal for me! So, I went back, but I sat all the way in the back of the church. I wanted to hear some more!

I really enjoyed the services and sermons at the Protestant church. I liked the idea of not portraying Jesus hanging on the cross. The explanation for that is that Jesus died on the cross, but He arose on the third day after His crucifixion and ascended into heaven and is sitting at the right hand of God the Father, not on a cross on a wall. I liked the fact that women did not have to wear veils and that they could become ordained ministers. There was much confusion concerning women in the clergy because of that Scripture where Paul said that women should remain silent in church (1st Corinthians 14:34). The truth is found in studying the Bible and not in personal interpretation of the Bible. One needs to look at the context to understand what Paul wrote to each church. Nonetheless, even before the church was formed, the first women to proclaim the Gospel were Mary Magdalene and the other Mary in Matthew 28:1-8. Needless to say, I liked the Protestant catechism and all the ministries in which the church members are involved.

During the course of one year, I joined various ministries and attended Bible study and Sunday worship services on a weekly basis. Everything was so exciting that I couldn't help but share my enthusiasm and my church stories with Art. Then, before one knew it, he started going to church with me. Of course, my mother-in-law was very happy. For one year, I went consistently, and my "whys" began to make sense. However, on a Palm Sunday in 1994, I found myself not going to church. This was shocking to my family. I had no explanation for why I wanted to stay home. I think they probably thought that I was going to be a backslider again. Scary thoughts!

I stayed home on that Palm Sunday; and for some strange reason, I started cleaning out the dresser drawers. All of a sudden, I looked at an old picture that was given to me a few years back. The picture's image (I still have It.) is an image of what we grew-up believing Christ to look like. I stopped what I was doing and stared at the picture and I swear that I felt His eyes staring at me, piercing through me. I don't know what came over me, but I got down on my knees and started crying and talking to the picture.

"You died for me." "Now I know why you died for me. Now I know what this Palm Sunday is all about! You died for me."

I felt as though buckets of tears were rolling down my face as I sobbed convulsively. This was the first time that I understood why Jesus carried the cross and bled on it. This time, I did not hear it from someone else; this time I understood it for myself as I felt the presence of God in that room. Herein is the main *why*. Herein was the true confession straight from my heart and directly to God. Herein was the day of my salvation. The Bible says, "*Because if you confess with your lips that Jesus is Lord and believe in your heart that God raised him from the dead, you will be saved. For one believes with the heart and so is justified, and one confesses with the mouth and so is saved*" (Romans 10:9-10) (NRSV) and there, you have it! My search had ended.

What I experienced in my room that day by myself is incredible and unbelievable. I felt and recognized the presence of God there with me. However, as I reflect on my past experiences, God has been present all along. I started getting flashbacks of the times when God used different things and people to get me out of trouble, like the time when I was almost mugged. As an unattached individual, I had the freedom to come and go as I pleased. I was divorced from my first husband and separated from my common-law husband. This was the time to "hang out" with my two so-called "friends"; in this situation, I was not thinking about church.

Girls' night out became a frequent getaway for the three of us. I do not remember who was giving us a ride back home after we left someone's apartment; but I do know that for some reason the driver had left something inside and told us to wait in his car while he went back inside the apartment. While we waited, some guy approached us. I noticed that he crept up to us and started staring at one of the women's gold chain. I looked him in the face and started talking. He kept inching his way closer and closer. It seemed that the closer he got, the more I talked. I was talking, but I noticed that he kept looking at her chain but also looking to the side while yet still paying attention to what I was saying. What am I talking about? Who knows! Does it matter? I all remember is that the next thing that happened is that he saw our driver approaching and said good-bye to us and dashed off. I knew his intentions were not good, and I believe that God used my tongue to delay him while our driver came back. It was the gift of gab that my heavenly Father has bestowed upon me that kept us from being mugged or possibly killed. As far as I was concerned, he could have been, as they say, "packing" a gun.

Of course, at the time, I had not arrived at the personal understanding that the hand of God is always ready to intervene. According to Romans 8:29-30, He already knew me before He called me, so He knew the trouble I was going to get into, and that is why He has always been there with me, waiting to step in and prevent worse things from happening to me. I won't say that everything was good but when I think about it, those things that I thought were bad could've been worse. And if bad things were not present, then how would I know that the good things are better with God's intervention? If not for the bad things, I would not be able to testify that God's presence helps me to overcome the bad things. Who knows but God what would have happened to me if He had not intervened all the times that I almost got raped, beaten, or probably even killed? He was watching me.

I have been in awkward situations plenty of times. I have been in the wrong places at the right time. Sound confusing? Well, I was in the wrong places because there was trouble in the wrong places, at the right time—it was the right time for God to teach a lesson. *"No testing has overtaken you that is not common to everyone. God is faithful, and he will not let you be tested beyond your strength, but with the testing he will also provide the way out so that you may be able to endure it"*(1st *Corinthians 10:13*) (NRSV). Since my salvation, I adopted this scripture as a personal testimony. I have come to the realization that I am constantly being tested by God, and that I have passed every test.

MyTambourine

I have not always been a worshiper. I grew up attending a "quiet" church where the Mass was mostly in Latin. That is one of the reasons why my *mami* would constantly pinch me or give me "the look." One, the Latin was funny to me and two, I could not sit still. There were no, "Amens" and "Hallelujahs," including falling out, running around the church, laying on of hands; and certainly, there was no speaking in tongues (other than the Latin). Mass was forty-five minutes long; that was it!

The furthest my praise went was to say *"ay Dios mio"* (Oh my God!). It is an expression that I used to indicate that something good happened that caused me to be grateful to God or that something happened that needed fixing, and that I knew it was God who would fix it. This is not to be confused with the OMG of nowadays when it is used for any old thing or any old reason and just merely to express oneself in an exaggerated manner. No, my "Oh my God" is expressed for my personal authentic experiences. I did not know it at that time, but one can say it is sort of a short prayer. It was (and continues to be), my confidence that somehow God is in the midst of whatever the situation may be.

Years after the quiet church, I found myself worshiping at services rendered in Spanish. The atmosphere was different. The music was more modern and choir members played guitars and tambourines. The service was livelier, and I thoroughly enjoyed it. The problem lies in the fact that I still did not conform to the entire rules and rituals that were customary in this particular denomination. Although the service was lively, I still did not quite understand what it meant to praise. I was still stuck in *"ay Dios mio"*!

The day when I finally realized what it means to praise God was that glorious day when I stopped what I was doing and started talking to God while sobbing convulsively, acknowledging His sacrifice for me. Days ahead, I kept getting flashbacks of the Spanish services where guitars and tambourines stirred up the rhythm in me, especially the tambourines. So here I am involved in several ministries, but since my favorite was the ministry of music, I joined two choirs. However, something was still missing. It was not until an anointing service consisting of laying on of hands, prophecy, running around the church, and falling out that I really yelled out my first praise. It was the moment when the desire to purchase a tambourine became engraved in my mind and spirit.

I purchased a tambourine with great joy. Of course, I do not know how to play it professionally, but my husband says that there is something about the way I play it that is different and uplifting. When I play my tambourine, I feel like I am in a different world, sort of like the seventh heaven. Nothing else around me matters. All I want to do is to shake and bang it when the choir sings so that God can hear me. I love God and appreciate all that God does for me, so why not make a joyful noise to praise and glorify Him? Why not praise God for delivering me from sin and from my abusers and for protecting me from something worse happening to me; for I realize that I won't complain; I mustn't complain, shouldn't complain, and that there is no need to complain, for I could have been six feet under. Why not praise Him in a way that also makes me feel good and it serves as a testimony to others? Nobody has to know exactly what is going on with you, but the mere expression of praise to God is sufficient to be an encouragement to somebody else.

Don't get me wrong—I don't just praise God with my tambourine. Not all of my praises call for me to play the tambourine. After all, will I be playing my tambourine while I am washing the dishes or sweeping the floor or better yet, while driving to the store? I believe that any expression of praise is pleasing to God, for the psalmist says in Psalm 107:1-2, *O give thanks to the Lord, for he is good; for his steadfast love endures forever. Let the redeemed of the Lord say so, those he redeemed from trouble.*

THE SHUSHERS

Praising my God with my tambourine reminds me of Moses' and Aaron's sister Miriam, and how she and her people were trapped at the Red Sea after being freed from bondage from the hands of Pharaoh. Pharaoh with his chariots went into the sea, (the Lord having allowed the waters to cover them). Yet, the Israelites crossed over on dryland. *"Then the prophet Miriam, Aaron's sister, took a tambourine in her hand; and all the women went out after her with tambourines and with dancing. And Miriam sang to them: 'Sing to the Lord, for he has triumphed gloriously; horse and rider he has thrown into the sea"* (Exodus 15:19-21) (NRSV).

Miriam and her people had a reason to praise God. The marvelous thing about their praise is that they were on one accord. They supported Miriam while she led them in song and dance. However, that was not the case for me for it did not take long before the enemy popped up his ugly head to try to discourage me from playing my tambourine.

When playing in a band or in a church choir, it is understandable to practice with the choir or the band, but when one is praising God, one, (at least I am), is in one's own world. It is just  the *Lord*, my tambourine, and me. At that moment, I am not worried or concerned about being in sync with the choir. Being in sync with God is what really matters, not what is going on around me. After years

46

of studying the Word, fasting, and praying; one's spiritual level should be as such that God, not a human, interprets our praises. We can hear more from God when we tune out all manner of distractions and pay attention to the Spirit.

This is my fourth tambourine. I donated the first one to my friend's church because it was round and huge, and it really did not feel right in my hand.

The second one broke during the time we were homeless (another story); the third one, I believe, I left at a church by mistake, though no one ever admitted to having seen it. The fourth one is in my bedroom.

It is the one pictured in this section. My tambourine attacks come at various times, places, and in various ways. What a joy to be able to praise God while the musician tickles the ivory and the choir lifts up the songs to God. But what a spiritual let-down when someone stops you after services to tell you specifically that you have ruined the song with your tambourine.

Yes, that my friends, was my first tambourine attack. Just picture me with a great big old smile on my face as I left the choir stand and someone cornered me just to tell me that I "messed up the song." Of course, as an infant Christian, all I did was cry my eyes out. I was dumbfounded and really embarrassed. I did not know how to defend myself. The next thing I knew, I was surrounded by other choir members who encircled me and prayed for me; and then, they followed up with telephone calls to check on me. Clearly, this was a significant spiritual attack when an infant Christian was not uplifted but was made to feel bad in her services to God.

There were several other instances in which I was confronted concerning my tambourine; but none were as tremendously powerful as the day when my praise became the talk of the campus eight years after the purchase of my first tambourine. How in the world was I supposed to stifle my praise after having inched up the highway to Wilberforce, Ohio in our old van, the PPT Van? Ah, the good old PPT Van, named after our church's devotional ministry: the Prayer and Praise Team (PPT). All the other cars and trucks were passing us like road runners (beep-beep) while we inched along like tortoises. My fight with the enemy continued as I went to give thanks to the Lord for carrying us up the mountains safely. It mattered not where I attended as long as I got my praise on!

Art and I visited a church where the atmosphere was quiet. Only a few clapped and a select few said "amen" ; then the rest of the worshipers looked as though they had arrived or something. That of course was not my concern; I just wanted to worship and praise in spite of who was there or who liked it or not. I felt all eyes upon me as I stayed at the altar the longest during altar call; then, silence was broken when the male chorus started singing, "What a Fellowship." Ah! A fast song! Oooooeeeeee! There went my tambourine like it had a life of its own, but it was a cause for commotion and gossip. After the service, the presiding prelate of that district approached me and told me that I was putting my life on the line there. Well, initially, his statement was confusing to me because I was thinking that he meant that I was putting my life on the line for going to seminary. But no— he rephrased his statement and said that I brought the fire from the 2nd Episcopal District, and that folks there did not praise and worship that way. Oh! Okay, but then a few minutes later the small group of praisers and clappers approached me and asked that I return and possibly join their choir because that type of praise was needed there. Oh my!

On my way back to our apartment, a student rushed over and told me that another student had ran over to tell her that some church folk told him that there was a woman who came to worship making a whole lot of noise and "shamangalanging" a tambourine. Strangely enough, it all seemed comical to me. I know that I had grown spiritually because I was not bothered by the comments. As a matter of fact, I welcomed the comments because it showed that they centered on my praise to God, who brought me through a lot of hardship and distress and delivered me from the hands of the enemy, which served as a testimony of God's divine favor upon me.

Well, the next week, Art and I visited another church, while another student visited the church we visited the first week. She told me that she fell into a deep sleep—so deep that she snored up a storm. I guess that if they gave her a blanket and a pillow she would have slept the whole week. When the service was over, she was asked how she enjoyed it. Her response was that she didn't because it was too quiet. She was told that another student had visited from the 2nd Episcopal District and made a whole lot of noise. They specified that they didn't do that type of "entertaining" there. Well, guess what, "I visited several churches until I found the right fit for me." And, the other student found a lively church that kept her awoke.

We visited that church one more time on Founder's Day. All the students were required to worship there. After the service, the pastor of the church approached me and offered her apologies to me, saying that she did not know "that"—I had been criticized. Ahhhh! It was so liberating to say these words: "Do not worry about it; that is water under the bridge." Understanding where others are in their spiritual lives and just concentrating on where one is in one's own spiritual life is a very liberating feeling and a sign of spiritual maturity.

For those who think that I make a whole lot of noise, I have come to the understanding that it is okay to make a whole lot of noise because the Bible says in a psalm of thanksgiving to, "Make a joyful noise to the Lord, all the earth" (Psalm 100:1) (NRSV), and to "Praise him with tambourine and dance" (Psalm 150:4) (NRSV). My noise-making happens during the songs that touch my soul. My noise-making is when the preacher preaches a soul-stirring, spirit-convicting sermon that causes me to say "Amen, "preach it pastor"; and "say it again, pastor"; "all right, pastor"; "hallelujah"; and "thank You, Jesus." The Holy Spirit dwells in me and is full of wisdom; and since the Holy Spirit lives in me, of course, I am not going to blurt out in the middle of a sentence or shake my tambourine while someone is talking; that's just plain rude. When others do that, it makes it harder on those of us who praise God in decency and in order.

I know life is not fair, but it is even more unfair when those of us who truly conduct ourselves in an appropriate manner get criticized because of someone else's immaturity. While a select few do not appreciate the tambourine, others do. Others become motivated to praise. I have heard others say that my tambourine playing gives them a sense of freedom. They see that I do not care who is looking or who doesn't like it. Years have passed, and I am no longer that scaredy-cat, baby Christian that cringes at the onset of the slightest spiritual "boo!" The Bible tells me that greater is He that is in me than he who is in the world (1 John 4:4).

There were several spiritual warfares: fear attacks, and threats. They invaded my praise to discourage me from playing the tambourine. After the campus drama, a physical ailment became the obstacle that temporarily prevented me from playing. How so? Nearly four years after graduating from seminary, I discovered a few bumps on my left thumb. I did not realize I had them because I had been very busy with course

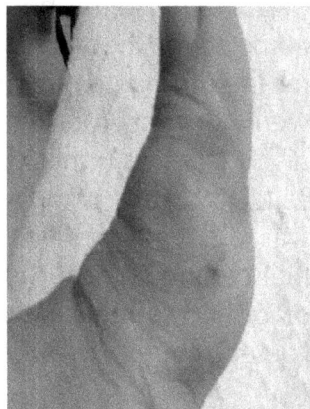

work, writing my first book, taking care of Art, church duties, and managing household matters; besides, I felt no pain in that area at all. Who REALLY pays that much attention to a thumb?

However, when it seemed as though not one more crumb could be added to my plate (no pun intended), a friend of mine invited me to lunch so that I might actually consume what was on my plate instead of what was on my plate consuming me. That is when I noticed the bumps on my left thumb. This was a cause for concern, so two days later I went to the emergency room. The doctor could not determine what the X-rays showed, so he diagnosed them as being fatty tumors, and he suggested that I go see an orthopedic hand specialist. Well, what could I do? I had no medical insurance and no time to take care of it.

So, life went on, the bumps grew, and I still kept playing my tambourine, but then, the bumps started spreading and hurting. Three years later, I was approved for medical insurance, so I made an appointment to see a medical doctor who told me that in her thirty years as a doctor, she had not seen anything like that; and that since she did not know what the bumps were, she was not accepting the "fatty tumors" diagnosis; hence, she referred me to an orthopedic hand surgeon who asked if I had smashed my thumb with anything metal. *Heavens to Murgatroyd!* Anything metal! Nooooo, what am I—a blacksmith? I could not think of any moment when I could have come in contact with anything metal. Surely, the tambourine was the furthest from my mind. The tumors had spread so far down my thumb that another micro inch would have damaged a nerve.

On August 6, 2013, I had the surgery that permanently removed the tumors. Of course, there is a medical term for them, but right now I want to finish this book; so I am not going to be bothered with looking for the discharge papers. The tumors were not cancerous. In the still of the night, I started thinking that all other "attacks" were petty compared to this one. Like the incident when I was told that I messed up the song, or that I needed to not play because that certain choir did not like tambourine playing, or when I was told that I had to rehearse with the choir, etc. etc., oh, and yes, when the "quiet" church members were indignant about the "entertainment"

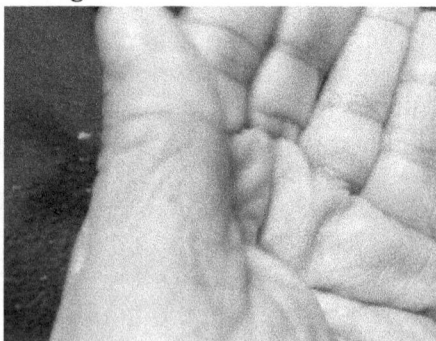

that I brought to their church; all of these things were petty, but to think that my nerves practically being damaged by years of "banging" on the tambourine was more than I could handle.

Eighteen years! Eighteen years of "shamangalanging" in honor of God. What now? He knows that it makes me happy to enter into His presence in music. So what am I going to do? For days and even weeks, I tossed and turned and thought and thought, and then it happened! At the crack of dawn, a verse from that familiar Scripture Psalm 15, flashed right through my mind, "Praise him with tambourine and dance" (Psalm 150:4).

DANCE!!!! Yes, I can do that. Not only was God telling me to move on and praise Him anyhow; He was also saying that I could dance my praise away with my new knee. Actually, I had two new knees. For over fifteen years I had been suffering with degenerative osteoarthritis in both knees. Because of the crookedness of my legs, I lost four inches from my height. Good grief, I was already short, at five-feet, one-inch tall. I almost had a heart attack when the doctor told me I had shrunk! From 2008 until 2013 I could hardly walk. In order to get things done around the house, I had to use Arthur's manual wheelchair.

I had total knee replacement on my left knee in November of 2013, and then on my right knee on January of 2014. I was told by my physical therapist that it takes one year for the thumb to heal; well, in the meantime, I had to praise God somehow, hallelujah anyhow!! So, I danced! I am at the point in my spiritual walk that if someone is not comfortable with my praise, then he or she needs to make an appointment with God because God is the One who created me the way HE wanted to create me. Above is a picture of one my new left knee; the right one is the same.

SNEAKY SAINTS

I cannot pinpoint a specific time when I desperately needed to praise the Lord more than when I was emotionally and spiritually attacked by a group of church folks whom I named "sneaky saints." No sooner did I overcome the tambourine attack when this particular group of church folks succeeded in stirring up my spiritual peace, but not my spiritual joy, because that is one thing that nobody can take away from me.

And so, my mind wanders back to that cold, rainy night; the type of rain that penetrates your bones and sends chills up your spine, when my mother-in-law and I returned to the church after visiting a dear friend, then discovered that there was no heat in the parsonage. I tried turning up the thermostat settings only to notice that nothing was happening. It was freezing cold and I had an elderly woman staying with me, so I went to check things out, only to discover that the locks on the church doors had been changed. Yes—changed! Why? How could this be, if five months prior, I was welcomed at this church with open arms? All smiles surrounded me as I thought I was in a safe place— a place of joy and peace. I came prepared for ministry. I was elated. I had just pastored a great group of people who were willing to take the church to a higher level to enter into a small church that was and continues to be comfortable with its "small church" mentality.

My goal was to reach out to this community where ignorance of Christ's redemptive power, substance abuse, domestic violence, single parenthood, and unchurched attitudes prevailed. It was a community very much similar to the one I grew up in the Lower East Side of Manhattan (LES) or *Loisaida,* as named by the Hispanics and Latinos.

This particular neighborhood brought back memories of the fifties where innocent childhood games made my soul merry. However, they were replaced in the '70s by scary moments that made my heart beat ferociously—scary moments when the daredevil boys would ride in backs of buses only to then jump in front of them. They were scary moments, when middle-school boys would ride on top of the elevators instead of riding *in* them. There were scary moments when drug dealers would yell out *"bajando"* (a Spanish cue that meant cops were "coming down the street.") And there were scary moments when I would dodge bullets as I walked down the avenue with my little boys. The Lower East Side, a place where, ten years later, the tagged-up hallways held the window panes where my neck would hang out in desperation while worrying about my teen age boys every time the gangs raided the block. The LES was the place where teenage girls were competing with each other to see who got pregnant first. The LES—the place where I was born and raised and had the courage to survive.

Bringing all the memories of the "hood" with me, I would go to this "new-to-me" city and make a difference. I would minister to the unchurched, the unsaved, the Hispanics, and the Latinos, the single parents, the substances abusers, the drug dealers, the un-wed mothers, the school drop outs, and anyone else who needed ministering to. I would take with me all the gifts and talents that my heavenly Father bestowed upon me. I would take with me my educational background, and I would take with me all the love and compassion that was in my heart. I was ready! But, all my ministry ideas would drip down the drain as they were interrupted by "Sneaky Saints."

I call them Sneaky Saints because although they smiled in my face, after two weeks of being there, they started slithering around and doing things behind my back. I noticed that there was a tightly knit bond among a couple of church officers and a handful of members. They would make church plans on their own without meeting with me. The most shocking discovery was when I found out that one of the married officers (I'll name her Sister S for "sneaky") was having an affair with another married officer (I'll name him "Brother S" for "sneaky"). Yes! It sounds like a soap opera. Of course, they were rumors that I could not readily confirm until that one unexpected moment when I surprised them alone.

It was during this time that Art was hospitalized for end-stage kidney failure. He was going back and forth between a hospital and a rehabilitation center for four months. He had a fever that would subside then start back up again. On this particular afternoon, before visiting Art, I received an unexpected telephone call. It was from Brother's wife, a woman who was much feared in the community. She asked if her husband was there at the church. Of course, I told her that I had to check. I informed her that I saw his truck and would notify him that she wanted to speak with him. I went down the stairs, only to discover that he was locked inside the church with Sister S. There was nothing to do in the church. It was clean, and there were no activities going on or business to conduct because I ran the office from the spare room in the parsonage.

So what were they doing? I do not know. All I know is that I knocked on the door and he came out. His lips were trembling and he really looked nervous. All of a sudden I heard a voice in the background. "Good morning, pastor!" With much excitement in her voice as if she were glad to see me, she spoke. That was quite strange because two days prior to that, she insulted me during a meeting. She threatened to leave the church and take with her whatever she had bought for the church. Then, the following day, she threatened me again, this time via e-mail. Why? All because I thought it was best for the choir to rehearse on non-Bible study days. Bible study was previously led by another preacher on Tuesdays, so on Wednesdays, they rehearsed. Since I became the pastor, I wanted to teach the congregation on Wednesdays and switch the choir rehearsal to Tuesdays.

Simply because I did not conform to her agenda, she began a campaign of lies to turn the members against me. That is when I noticed how they changed, openly and dramatically. At first, they would whisper among themselves; but now, they confronted me and undermined my authority. They refused to attend Bible study, Sunday school, men's Bible study, and the women's fellowship that I had initiated. Only three faithful members would show up for Bible study and Sunday school, two men for the men's Bible study and one lady for the women's fellowship. As for Brother S., I heard that every time he got mad at a pastor, he left the church and stopped supporting it. This time was no different.

At first I tried to justify Sister S's behavior due to her dependency on OxyContin and various other medications. However, the image of Judas Iscariot flashed in my mind as he agreed to betray Jesus. It is the best way to describe how I perceive her now. All along, she has been pulling the wool over my eyes. She has been pleasing me to gain my confidence—"pastor this" and "pastor that." Her threat was that if she left the church, the church would fall apart. She managed to convince her group to turn against me. That is when I had that "aha" moment when I realized that Sister S had been a phony all along. All of a sudden her smile had a forced look, and her face looked distorted.

Since the church was not a retreat for fornicators, I called a meeting with the leadership. I communicated my findings and apparently they disregarded my statement. I believe they turned a deaf ear to my discussion when I related my decision to change the church locks. It was clear that their agenda was to make my life miserable to the point that I would give up and leave. My next step was to meet with the trustees to purchase the locks. The trustees agreed and two of them escorted me to the hardware store. They purchased and changed the locks. When the stewards found out, they were appalled and questioned my authority.

According to them, I had not consulted with them. Since Sister S had turned them against me, this incident served to make matters worse. The treasurer resigned. The head steward refused to sign all checks and no bills were paid. They completely turned their backs on me while leaving me with just three supporting members who were not influential enough to stand up against them. The conspiracy continued as they invited other preachers to the pulpit to preach without consulting me.

On the Good Friday before I left the church, I was assigned the first Word: "Father, forgive them." Strange! Right? There was nothing I could do because I did not want to embarrass any of the guest preachers. The stewards organized a repast. It was at this moment that I realized how really evil these persons were. After the service, I had planned to visit Art at the hospital. But, believe it or not, even though I had not eaten all day long, no plate was set aside for me. As a matter of fact, as the others ate, the head steward threw the rest of the food in the trash right in front of my face. The only reason why I ate that night was because one of the members prepared a meal of jasmine rice and black beans. The black beans were so delicious that I asked for the recipe, but her response was, "I didn't do anything to the beans, just rinsed them from the can and heated them up so that you could eat." It was the best meal anyone could ever eat because it was prepared, not with herbal spices but with the spices of love and compassion.

While Arthur was in the rehabilitation center, it was this same lovely lady who opened her home to me so that as I walked out of that church, I could walk into her home and stay as long as I needed to. She was my prayer partner then and continues to be now as I write this in 2014. It was in this lovely lady's house that my mother-in-law and I visited on that rainy night. We had a wonderful time eating Chinese food and just sitting around talking. What a perfect evening until we headed back to the parsonage to find that the heat had been turned off and the church's locks had been changed.

You are probably saying that there is more to this than meets the eye. Well, you are right. There is so much to tell, but one other incident that occurred that I feel necessary to tell is the day we celebrated Friends and Family Day. The guest church raised $900 back in their town prior to the service to jump-start the service. What is strange is that it was placed in an envelope, handed over to me during the welcoming of the visitors, and then I handed it over to the steward. Well, believe it or not, that envelope went "missing." The head steward to whom I handed the envelope came knocking at the parsonage at eight in the evening, all excited and out of breath.

The steward said: "Do you know where the envelope is?"
I said: "Envelope? What envelope?"

The steward said, "The envelope with the $900!"

I said, "I gave it to you!"

The steward said, "Well, we looked all over and can't find it."

The money was never found. I reported the incident to the police and the insurance company. The church was reimbursed $500. When the check arrived, I deposited it in the bank and that caused a major uproar. That is when I found out that they did not allow any pastor to conduct bank transactions because they did not trust any pastor. According to them, a former pastor embezzled money from the church's account for personal gain. They organized it so that the three signatures on the checks did not include the pastor's signature. In order for a pastor to be included in the signatures, the three had to agree and go to the bank with the pastor, and of course, they did not want that to happen. So, they organized a meeting to gang up on me for depositing the check.

Yes, I was spiritually wounded. It was a test of my faith and a test of my calling. But, then, I realized that it was not about me, but it was all about the things that they did. In my eyes all the things they did were underhanded and despicable, especially since they professed to be Christians. It was this experience with this particular group of people that helped me to decide to be more careful in whom I placed my trust.

Since that incident, I worked diligently on my first book, *"Pleas, Praises and Promises,"* a devotional centered on the book of Psalms. Writing "Pleas, Praises, and Promises" helped me to overcome the hurt, pain, and bitterness of all my past experiences. I was subjected to sexual, physical, emotional, and spiritual abuse. Yet, I did not break me because my strength, encouragement, and hope for the future were found in God's Word.

EPILOGUE

Arriving at the point where one is able to forgive even when the offender has never apologized is an amazing place to be. And one should never use the word *never* while folks are alive, because one never knows if and when that person might actually have the opportunity or have a change a heart to be able to apologize. But, when they have passed, you can say never because they are no longer alive, and they didn't apologize. For those who are still alive and have not apologized, I can say, they have not YET apologized because they are still here and perhaps they are reading this. It is never too late to apologize and never too late to accept an apology, forgive, and move on. In my case, it matters not whether those who are still living apologize or not. I have found peace by silently forgiving them a long time ago. An apology is not necessary because that is between them and God. I have removed myself from the picture. I have found peace in blessing those who cursed me and praying for those who abused me (Luke 6:28).

Since I want my heavenly Father to forgive me when I sin, then I need to forgive others when they sin against me, regardless of what that sin is. We reach a certain spiritual level when we do not allow someone's non-apologetic behavior to affect us. You might call this strange or may possibly not agree with me at this present time, but a few years ago, unfortunately, I happened to end up in the same place at the same time with the Stomper. Remember him? It was one of those occasions that we simply could not avoid. But guess what? Although the opportunity to ask for my forgiveness was staring dead into his face, he didn't, and somehow it did not bother me. Hmmm! Then, years later, we needed to be in the same place at the same time again. You might not agree with me, but this time I hugged him and asked how he was doing. I really did not feel anything. I do not feel hatred or bitterness or the need to seek revenge. Yes, he had trespassed against me, abused me physically and emotionally, and hadn't apologized; however, I had silently forgiven him. I had reached that certain level of spirituality—that place where an apology is no longer necessary for me to move on. My focus has shifted from dwelling on what those persons did to me to how I can better myself because of what was done to me.

ANALYSIS

When I think about Jesus hanging there on the cross of Golgotha stripped of his outer garment, by the guards; I can't help but identify with some of His pain. I believe He was indeed molested for the story is told that He was stripped and the guards gambled for His clothes. Stripped, humiliated, and shamed—YET, Jesus forgave them. For when Jesus said "Father, forgive them" (Luke 23:34), the "them" includes all those who offended Him by questioning His identity in Matthew 4:3; calling Him a liar in Matthew 9:3; taunting him in Matthew 27:44; and in John 1:11, he was rejected by His own people. In John 7:20, He was even accused of being demon-possessed.

This book is not a Bible study or a collection of sermons, but about how I, in spite of all the years of pain and bitterness, have managed to forgive the persons mentioned here who have offended me verbally, sexually, physically, emotionally, and/or even spiritually.

When I look at the author and finisher of my life, and how He being the Son of God, forgave all His offenders, who am I that I should not do the same? No one has or will ever endure the pain and suffering as Jesus did; but the degree of bitterness and pain is measured according to what each individual can bear. I am not alone in this battle against all types of abuse, and I hope and pray that those persons who have been hurt in any way understand that many people abuse their authority. I believe that they are on a power trip. Perhaps, it is their inadequacy. They lack something. Have you ever wondered that your mere presence intimidated others? There is something about you that others can't handle? Perhaps, you are prettier than they or perhaps you are smarter. Perhaps people like you more than they like them. You were born with an anointing that they cannot handle, and they do not even know what it is.

"Indeed, we live as human beings, but we do not wage war according to human standards for the weapons of our warfare are not merely human, but they have divine power to destroy strongholds. We destroy arguments and every proud obstacle raised up against the knowledge of God, and we take every thought captive to obey Christ" (2 Corinthians 10:35) (NRSV).

Non-Biblical Quotes

"To err is human, to forgive, divine."—Alexander Pope

"Throughout life people will make you mad, disrespect you and treat you bad. Let God deal with the things they do, cause hate in your heart will consume you too."
—Will Smith

"Forgiveness has nothing to do with absolving a criminal of his crime. It has everything to do with relieving oneself of the burden of being a victim--letting go of the pain and transforming oneself from victim to survivor."
—C.R. Strahan

"As I walked out the door toward the gate that would lead to my freedom, I knew if I didn't leave my bitterness and hatred behind, I'd still be in prison."
—Nelson Mandela

"To love means loving the unlovable. To forgive means pardoning the unpardonable. Faith means believing the unbelievable. Hope means hoping when everything seems hopeless."

—G.K. Chesterton

"Forgiveness means it finally becomes unimportant that you hit back. You're done. It doesn't necessarily mean that you want to have lunch with the person. If you keep hitting back, you stay trapped in the nightmare...."

—Anne Lamott, *Plan B: Further Thoughts on Faith*

All quotes taken from https://www.goodreads.com/quotes/tag/forgiveness

CHAPTER SIX

LETTERS OF FORGIVENNES

. . . .

TO THE ROLLING STONE (R.I.P.

Abuelo, you attempted to rape me two times; however, I forgive you seventy-seven times seven (77 x 7) as ordered by Jesus in Matthew 18:21, 22. Two for the two times that I am aware of and seventy-five times for the seventy-five times you might have been tempted. Although you were my abuelo, you were still a man endowed with desires and temptations. One way that I overcame the trauma from even thinking of possibly being raped by you is found in the second chapter of 1 John verse 16; which assures me that the flesh is full of lust and so are the eyes; and that the pride of life is not of God but of this sinful world.

A grandfather is one we should look up to for love, protection, and to spoil us, not spoil our bodies or our minds or our emotions and cause fear and confusion. Yes, fear and confusion are the inheritance you left me with. I left those two incidents buried in my mind. My lips have been sealed for too long. The silence is now broken as I penned my feelings so that other victims may gain courage and speak up.

Yes, I could go on through life holding a grudge, rejoicing in your death, wishing that my genes were unrelated to yours; and of course, ultimately, not forgiving you, but that is not the case because the Bible tells me that if I forgive others their trespasses, my heavenly Father will also forgive me (Matthew 6: 14) and since I fall short of the glory of God (Romans 3:23), I most certainly need for Him to forgive me, so because of that, I forgave you a long time ago because you could not help yourself. You are gone but there are others like you who are still living, so to them I write what the Word says:

"Blessed is the man that endures temptation: for when he is tried, he shall receive the crown of life, which the Lord has promised to them that love him" (James 1:12) (NKJV).

"Watch and pray, that you enter not into temptation: the spirit indeed is willing, but the flesh is weak" (Matthew 26:41). (NKJV).

"Submit yourselves therefore to God. Resist the devil, and he will flee from you" (James 4:7) (KJV).

To Manteco (R.I.P.)

Letting me cry all night, as a baby, beating me unfairly, and wounding me with your words, left an impact on my life as a child, teenager, and adult. For years, I considered myself to be a disorganized individual. It has been horrible. Every time I misplace something, I think of those words that pierced right through my heart; "tu nunca te fijas" ('you never focus.')" For the longest time, mami, I was afraid to bake a cake. The thought of it flopping was terrifying to me. I guess I associated flopping with failing. To me, the mere thought of failing at anything was disturbing, saddening, and unthinkable.

Sixty-two years have passed, and I have never met the man you fell in love with and sent away. Did I have resentment towards him or you and anyone else who knew? Have I wondered at times if Angel ever even bothered to ask about me? Did I ever say to myself, I wish my biological father would have raised me? Did I blame you? Yes, I have and I did; past tense. It took years to forgive and be content with simply not knowing. It took years of deciding to stop searching. This is in the past tense because I finally realized that I had a Father all along: God. God is the best Father any person could ever have. God has never left me, nor forsaken me. He has never put me down. Most of all, God loved me so much that he gave his only Son, so that I may not perish but have eternal life. (John 3:16). All I had to do was believe in Him. That's all! I did not have to bake any perfect cakes. When I goofed up, He would chastise me but not with an extension cord or a belt. And when He forgave me, He covered the scars not with VapoRub but with love. Your job, mami, was to love, train, teach, and direct me, not discipline me in anger. I do thank you for finding a way to give me a name, but I would have loved to see more of love in that household than anger and strictness. I have forgiven you, so rest in peace.

To the Window Watcher (R.I.P)

Papi, as you took on the task of adopting and raising me, your job was, alongside my mami, to protect, provide, teach, and love me as a father would love a child, not as a man would a woman. The nights that you entered my room were frightening nights. I did not know what you were going to do. Those images of you standing there by the window have weighed heavily on my little girl's brain throughout my childhood. As I blossomed into a young lady, I felt self-conscious about that one part of my body that you did touch; my thighs.

You, Abuelo and Tio Pablo, contributed to my distrust in men. I could not see that a man would love me for me rather than for what he could just get from my body. I kept all of that and the nightmares to myself because I thought that if I said something that I would be blamed and beaten, and you knew perfectly well that my mami would beat me for the slightest things.

No, the subject never came up, and you never did admit what you did; nonetheless, the God in me let me see the good in you. I saw that it mattered not that I was someone else's biological child for you to consider me your own child. For that, I thank you, and by the way, once I understood the good in you, I forgave you; I forgave you—years ago. May you rest in peace.

"Food is meant for the stomach and the stomach for food,
and God will destroy both one and the other. The body is meant not
for fornication but for the Lord, and
the Lord for the body" (1st Corinthians 6:13) (NRSV)

To Scarface (Fate Unknown)

For years, I wondered if you ever attempted to know my whereabouts or even bothered to ask about me. I wondered what you looked like and what type of job you had. I wondered why you were jumped in an alley. I walked up and down Ludlow Street looking for a man with a scar. I hoped to meet my aunts in my latter years so that I may get some closure. Perhaps they would say something to me. They had talked to my mami, and they had seen me several times. Why didn't they approach me? I wondered for years if I would ever meet you. I wondered for years what my brothers and sisters were like. I agonized over the thought that I had a father who did not search for me. You knew that I existed but did nothing about it. You did not physically, sexually, or spiritually abuse me, but you did emotionally. And to me, that also was an unforgivable act; but I forgave you even though I do not know if you thought you needed forgiveness. I really think it does not matter if I meet you or not at this point because God has been my real Father. I spent a lot of years wondering if you ever thought about me; or if you were ever sorry about not meeting me; or if you even thought of meeting me; or if it bothered you that you never met me.

Those days are over because since I matured I no longer place so much emphasis on wondering because Matthew 23:9 tells me that I am to call no one my father on earth for I have one Father—the One in heaven. That brings me comfort because I know that every time that you were not there, according to Philippians 4:19, which is my second favorite Scripture, God has been there to fully satisfy every need of mine according to His riches in glory in Christ Jesus. No more wondering. No more hoping. It is okay because I learned from Paul the apostle in Romans 8:37 that I am more than a conqueror through Christ who loved me. And, wherever my paternal siblings are, I pray that they have had a wonderful life.

To Sister Sticky Fingers (Fate Unknown)

There is not much that I want to say to you, except as a teacher, your job was to teach and encourage. You don't have to like a student, but you must perform your duty as an educator. Teaching is not chalking your ego or exercising your power or abusing your authority to teach. You, as a servant of God, should conduct yourself in a manner that is pleasing to God so that your students may follow your example. As a teacher in a parochial school, you should know that the Bible speaks to teachers in this manner:

> "Show yourself in all respects a model of good works, and in your teaching show integrity, gravity, and sound speech that cannot be censured; then any opponent will be put to shame, having nothing evil to say of us" (Titus 2:7,8) (NRSV).

Making the children empty their book bags in front of their classmates because you felt that the contents did not meet your expectations of neatness or forcing them to bend over to hit them with a ruler because they looked at you crooked or even sending them to the bathroom to wash their mouths out with soap because of something they said is not my idea of an effective teacher. Grounding me from seeing that classic movie The Sound of Music, as much as I love music, was worse than being hit with a belt for no particular reason. You, madam, have not been an example of a teacher that I would ever model after. No, I never heard from you again. The last time I inquired as an adult, I heard that you were no longer at that school. And if by chance you suffered from OCD, I hope that you received some help along the way.

To Mrs. Sticky Fingers (Fate Unknown)

What you did was scary and humiliating. Those sensations that you tried to arouse in me were not supposed to be from one female to another, especially from a seasoned woman to a young blossoming woman. You have a daughter. Have you stopped to think how she would feel if a friend of yours would have done that to her? You, ma'am, besides attempting to commit an unnatural act of nature, have defiled your husband's bed. This is what the Bible says to married persons, including you: Let marriage be held in honor by all, and let the marriage bed be kept undefiled; for God will judge fornicators and adulterers (Hebrews 13:4).

Even if you didn't have your way with me, it's the thought that counts. You thought you could overpower me, but I have news for you—I have more power than you can ever imagine for the mere fact of getting away from your advances and gaining the victory; I have overcome. Fleeing from you is not a sign of weakness but a sign of not allowing your measly power to overtake me. The spiritual power that I have comes from God, and it overcomes your physical power that comes from the devil, so guess what? I win! Now, my victory comes from forgiving you because when I didn't forgive you, it happened again, and I certainly do not wish this to happen to me again: a third time. Forgiving you is freeing me and making me stronger so that I will never fall into anyone's trap ever again. So ma'am, because I have forgiven you, I can now write about it peacefully.

To the Stomper

"Love is patient; love is kind; love is not envious or boastful or arrogant or rude. It does not insist on its own way; it is not irritable or resentful; it does not rejoice in wrongdoing, but rejoices in the truth. It bears all things, believes all things, hopes all things, endures all things" (1 Corinthians 13:4-8) (NRSV).

"The Lord tests the righteous and the wicked, and his soul hates the lover of violence". (Psalm 11:5) (NRSV).

The way you treated me in no way shape or form is called love, and no, sir, you have not apologized to me, and it has been over forty years. Do not worry. I do not need an apology from you because of your lack of love for me I have learned to give thanks to the God of heaven for His steadfast love endures forever (Psalm 136:26). And, because God loves me so much, twenty-three years later, He sent me someone who loves me for me and who has never laid a hand on me. As of 2014, we have been married for twenty-three years. Hmmm, twenty-three and twenty-three! I wonder if that might have some significance.

To Ms. Sticky Fingers (R.I.P.)

My question to you is did you ever see me as a person in need of your help? Or as a woman you could help yourself too? If the latter were your initial intentions, then you must have skipped over the story of Sodom and Gomorrah (Genesis 19:1-29. Your inappropriate behavior toward me and my rejecting your advances cost me my jobs; but the way I see it, I was not born to do the same work you did. You had one plan for me, but God had another plan for me. I was devastated when you refused to take me to work, God said don't worry, for surely I know the plans I have for you, says the Lord, plans for your welfare and not for harm, to give you a future with hope (Jeremiah 29:11).

Well, here I am twenty-five years later (2014), an ordained minister and working on my doctorate. Even though you intended me harm, God intended it for good in order to preserve a numerous people as He is doing today (Genesis 50:20). Oh, and yes, though you never apologized, it is fine; I did not need you to apologize. I forgave you, and I moved on.

For those who are still living and have the same intentions as this lady did, let me remind you of a Scripture to live by: *"You shall not lie with a male as with a woman it is an abomination"* (Leviticus 18:22) (NRSV).

To My Long-Lost BFF

Some friends play at friendship but a true friend sticks closer than one's nearest kin (Proverbs 18:24). Many proclaim themselves loyal, but who can find one worthy of trust? (Proverbs 20:6). A friend loves at all times and kinsfolk are born to share adversity. (Proverbs 17:17), and you my friend, without any explanation, walked out of my life when I needed you the most. All I wanted to know was WHY? Because of your abandonment, I continued on with life without ever seeking a BFF because I was afraid of getting left again. But that is okay because I am over it, and I do not need to know why.

After wasting nearly thirty-six years focusing on where you were and the why of your abandonment, I recently found out that you were alive and well. Well, guess what, so am I because the Spirit of the Lord is upon me because he has anointed me to bring good news to the poor. He has sent me to proclaim release to the captives and recovery of sight to the blind, to let the oppressed go free, to proclaim the year of the Lord's favour (Luke 4:18-19). I did not know then, but as I matured and stopped thinking about you less and less, I came to the understanding that God was, is, and will still be my BFF because God was, is and always will be my refuge and my strength and a very present help in trouble. (Psalm 6:1), and he has kept His promise, and that is sufficient for me.

To All BFFs

It is not enough to cut one's fingers as a blood pact or follow any initiation process to be loyal forever. No, we need to be there for each other in the good and bad times. I did not know it at that time, but the Bible says to bear one another's burdens, and in this way you will fulfill the law of Christ (Galatians 6.2). A mere childhood ritual is not going to suffice unless we carry it throughout our lives together. We have grown up now, and life is not a game; and if we truly love our BFFs, then we need to think back and honor our promises to each other so that we can truly say to each other "I've got your back."

To the Head Slapper (R.I.P.)

It really doesn't matter to me that you carried your Bible everywhere and said you knew the Word; you must have missed the scripture that says that I am a child of God (John 1:12). *"Before the foundation of the world I was chosen to be holy and blameless before him in love"* (Ephesians 1:4). *"I am fearfully and wonderfully made"* (Psalm 139:14), and that is why I am the head and not the tail, only at the top and not at the bottom (Deuteronomy 28:13). *I am the salt of the earth* (Matthew 5:13) and the light of the world (Matthew 5:14). I produce good works because I am God's workmanship (Ephesians 2:10); and am more than a conqueror through him who loved me (Romans 8:37). What you did was wrong; you brought me down, yet you never apologized. Although for years I wanted to retaliate, I listened to what is written in Romans 12: 19-20 *"Beloved, never avenge yourselves, but leave room for the wrath of God; for it is written, 'Vengeance is mine, I will repay, says the Lord. Oh, how much easier it is to give my hurts to the Lord than to try to do all that work myself")* (NRSAV).

To the Money Grabber

No, we were not biological sisters; however, I considered us sisters indeed. For many years, I called you my sister, not even my half-sister, but my sister because I considered you my family. You stopped coming around, and I could not figure out why. I was too young to go visit you on my own. Later on, your daughter wanted me to be godmother to your grandson, and then all of a sudden she changed her mind. I do not know why. I do not know what went down, and it would have been good to know at that time what was troubling you. I do not hold that against you because you just could not handle the fact that my father, yes, my father took care of my mami (his legitimate wife) and me. That was not my fault. Everywhere he went, he would say I was his daughter. Well, that is true. I called him my father for 14 years until I knew the truth, then I still called him father. That is what family is about: love, respect, and gratitude.

> *"Do nothing from selfish ambition or conceit, but in humility regard others as better than yourselves. Let each of you look not to your own interests, but to the interests of others" (Philippians 2:3-4)* (NRSV).

To the Sneaky Saints

I am inclined to believe that you are probably not worried about me or even thinking about me; but just in case you wondered what was going on in my mind then and what is going on in my mind now, just know this—when you turned your backs on me, and I thought I couldn't go on. God said, *"My grace is sufficient for you, for power is made perfect in weakness. So, I will boast all the more gladly of my weaknesses, so that the power of Christ may dwell in me"* (2nd Corinthians 12:9) (NRSV). I took that unfortunate brief time we spent together as a learning experience and a time to appreciate God more. You probably did not think you did anything wrong or probably felt that you did not need to apologize. Although, you never apologized, it is okay. You do not need to apologize for me to forgive you because I have already forgiven you. I do not harbor ill feelings toward you.

> *"And this is my prayer, that your love may overflow more and more with knowledge and full insight to help you to determine what is best, so that in the day of Christ you*

may be pure and blameless, having produced the harvest of righteousness that comes through Jesus Christ for the glory and praise of God" (Philippians 1:9-11) (NRSV).

"Finally, all of you, have unity of spirit, sympathy, love for one another, a tender heart, and a humble mind. Do not repay anyone evil for evil, but take thought for what is noble in the sight of all. If it is possible, so far as it depends on you, live peaceably with all. Beloved, never avenge yourselves, but leave room for the wrath of God; for it is written, 'Vengeance is mine, I will repay' says the Lord. No, 'if your enemies are hungry, feed them; if they are thirsty, give them something to drink; for by doing this you will heap burning coals on their head.' Do not be overcome by evil, but overcome evil with good" (Romans 12:17-21) (NRSV).

After a short period of pastoring, this is what I learned as I reflected upon our interaction as children of God and workers in his kingdom:

"As God's chosen ones, holy and beloved, clothe yourselves with compassion, kindness, humility, meekness, and patience. Bear with one another and, if anyone has a complaint against another, forgive each other; just as the Lord has forgiven you, so you also must forgive. Above all, clothe yourselves with love, which binds everything together in perfect harmony" (Colossians 3:12-14) (NRSV).

"We then who are strong ought to bear with the scruples of the weak and" (Romans 15:1-2) (NKJV).
"Do not rejoice when your enemies fall, and do not let not your heart be glad he stumbles" (Proverbs 24:17) (NKJV).

"Love one another with mutual affection; outdo one another in showing honor" (Romans 12:10) (NRSV).

"For we are his workmanship, created in Christ Jesus for good works, which God prepared beforehand, that we should walk in them" (Ephesians 2:10) (KJV).

Therefore, as we have opportunity, let us do good to all, especially to those who are of the household of faith. (Galatians 6:10) (NKJV).

And be kind to one another, tenderhearted, forgiving one another, even as God in Christ forgave you. (Ephesians 4:32) (NKJV).

"Be angry, and do not sin": do not let the sun go down on your wrath. (Ephesians 4:26) (NKJV).

CHAPTER SEVEN

Procedures for Moving Beyond Bitterness

FROM THIS DAY FORWARD

In dealing with any type of abuse that causes you to think negative thoughts or feelings that are not recorded in God's word, write these scriptures on the notepad of your mind:

"Whenever you may think you can't bear something; God has already said you can do all things through him who strengthens you" (Philippians 4:13) (NRSV).

"Whenever you think that things are impossible: God already said that what is impossible for mortals is possible for God" (Luke 18:27) (NRSV).

"Whenever you may think you are condemned: God already said there is therefore now no condemnation for those who are in Christ Jesus" (Romans 8:1) (NRSV).

"Whenever you may think nothing good can come out of a bad situation, God has already said, that All things work together for good for those who love God, who are called according to his purpose" (Romans 8:28) (NRSV).

"Whenever you think you are all alone: God already said that He will never leave you or forsake you" (Hebrews 13:5) (NRSV).

"Whenever you may think you are afraid: God already said that He has not given you a spirit of cowardice, but rather a spirit of power and of love and of self-discipline" (2 Timothy 1:7) (NRSV).

"Whenever you may think you are worried and frustrated: God already said, 'Casting all care upon Him, for He careth for you" (1 Peter 5:7) (NKJ).

.

GOD AND YOU

YOU: *"Be pleased, O God, to deliver me. O Lord, make haste to help me!" (Psalm 70:1)* (NRSV).

GOD: *"Call on me in the day of trouble; I will deliver you, and you shall glorify me" (Psalm 50:15)* (NRSV).

YOU: *"Let those be put to shame and confusion who seek my life. Let those be turned back and brought to dishonor who desire to hurt me" (Psalm 70:2)* (NRSV).

GOD: *"Whoever does not abide in me is thrown away like a branch and withers; such branches are gathered, thrown into the fire, and burned. If you abide in me, and my words abide in you, ask for whatever you wish, and it will be done for you" (John 15.6-7)* (NRSV).

YOU: *"Let those who say, "Aha, Aha!" turn back because of their shame" (Psalm 70:3)* (NRSVA).

GOD: *"Do you not know that wrongdoers will not inherit the kingdom of God? Do not be deceived! Fornicators, idolaters, adulterers, male prostitutes, sodomites, thieves, the greedy, drunkards, revilers, robbers—none of these will inherit the kingdom of God" (1st Corinthians 6:9-10)* (NRSV).

"Do not fear, for I am with you, do not be afraid, for I am your God; I will strengthen you, I will help you, I will uphold you with my victorious right hand" (Isaiah 41:10) (NRSV).

YOU

"I will give thanks to you, O Lord, among the peoples, and I will sing praises to you among the nations. For your steadfast love is higher than the heavens, and your faithfulness reaches to the clouds" (Psalm 108:3, 4) (NRSV).

YOUR TESTIMONY

"I sought the Lord, and he answered me, and delivered me from all my fears (Psalm 34:4); in God I trust; I am not afraid. What can a mere mortal do to me? (Psalm 56:11). For God alone my soul waits in silence, for my hope is from him. He alone is my rock and my salvation, my fortress; I shall not be shaken. On God rests my deliverance and my honor; my mighty rock, my refuge is in God (Psalm 62:5). The Lord is my strength and my shield; in him my heart trusts; so I am helped, and my heart exults, and with my song I give thanks to him (Psalm 28:7). I bless the Lord who gives me counsel; in the night also my heart instructs me (Psalm 16:7). Surely goodness and mercy shall follow me all the days of my life, and I shall dwell in the house of the Lord my whole life long" (Psalm 23:6) (NRSV).

FROM GOD TO ALL

"When they call to me, I will answer them; I will be with them in trouble, I will rescue them and honor them (Psalm 91:15). After this manner therefore pray ye: Our Father which art in heaven, Hallowed be thy name. Thy kingdom come, Thy will be done in earth, as it is in

heaven. Give us this day our daily bread. And forgive us our debts, as we forgive our debtors. And lead us not into temptation, but deliver us from evil: For thine is the kingdom, and the power, and the glory, forever. Amen (Matthew 6:9-13, KJV).

GODLY ADMONITION
Ephesians 5:1-6:4

"Therefore be imitators of God, as beloved children, 2 and live in love, as Christ loved us and gave himself up for us, a fragrant offering and sacrifice to God. 3 But fornication and impurity of any kind, or greed, must not even be mentioned among you, as is proper among saints. 4 Entirely out of place is obscene, silly, and vulgar talk; but instead, let there be thanksgiving. 5 Be sure of this, that no fornicator or impure person, or one who is greedy (that is, an idolater), has any inheritance in the kingdom of Christ and of God. 6 Let no one deceive you with empty words, for because of these things the wrath of God comes on those who are disobedient. 7 Therefore do not be associated with them. 8 For once you were darkness, but now in the Lord you are light. Live as children of light—9 for the fruit of the light is found in all that is good and right and true. 10 Try to find out what is pleasing to the Lord. 11 Take no part in the unfruitful works of darkness, but instead expose them. 12 For it is shameful even to mention what such people do secretly; 13 but everything exposed by the light becomes visible, 14 for everything that becomes visible is light. Therefore it says, Sleeper, awake! Rise from the dead, and Christ will shine on you.' 15 Be careful then how you live, not as unwise people but as wise, 16 making the most of the time, because the days are evil. 17 So do not be foolish, but understand what the will of the Lord is. 18 Do not get drunk with wine, for that is debauchery; but be filled with the Spirit, 19 as you sing psalms and hymns and spiritual songs among yourselves, singing and making melody to the Lord in your hearts,

20 giving thanks to God the Father at all times and for everything in the name of our Lord Jesus Christ. 21 Be subject to one another out of reverence for Christ. 22 Wives, be subject to your husbands as you are to the Lord. 23 For the husband is the head of the wife just as Christ is the head of the church, the body of which he is the Saviour. 24 Just as the church is subject to Christ, so also wives ought to be, in everything, to their husbands. 25 Husbands, love your wives, just as Christ loved the church and gave himself up for her, 26 in order to make her holy by cleansing her with the washing of water by the word, 27 so as to present the church to himself in splendour, without a spot or wrinkle or anything of the kind—yes, so that she may be holy and without blemish. 28 In the same way, husbands should love their wives as they do their own bodies. He who loves his wife loves himself. 29 For no one ever hates his own body, but he nourishes and tenderly cares for it, just as Christ does for the church, 30 because we are members of his body. 31 'For this reason a man will leave his father and mother and be joined to his wife, and the two will become one flesh.' 32 This is a great mystery, and I am applying it to Christ and the church. 33 Each of you, however, should love his wife as himself, and a wife should respect her husband. Children, obey your parents in the Lord, for this is right. 2 'Honour your father and mother'—this is the first commandment with a promise: 3 'so that it may be well with you and you may live long on the earth.' 4 And, fathers, do not provoke your children to anger, but bring them up in the discipline and instruction of the Lord" (NRSV).

FROM GOD TO THE UNGODLY

"Now the works of the flesh are evident: sexual immorality, impurity, sensuality, idolatry, sorcery, enmity, strife, jealousy, fits of anger, rivalries, dissensions, divisions, envy, drunkenness, orgies, and things like these. I warn you, as I warned you before, that those who do such things will not inherit the kingdom of God (Galatians 5:19-21). Put

to death, therefore, whatever in you is earthly: fornication, impurity, passion, evil desire, and greed (which is idolatry) (Colossians 3:5). But as for the cowardly, the faithless, the detestable, as for murderers, the sexually immoral, sorcerers, idolaters, and all liars, their portion will be in the lake that burns with fire and sulfur, which is the second death (Revelation 21:8) (NRSV).

Whenever you think you are all alone:

STOP!!!!!

—If you have ever physically sexually, emotionally and/or spiritually abused anyone in your life,

—If you have ever even thought about physically, sexually, emotionally and/or spiritually abusing anyone in your life,

—If you are thinking about physically, sexually, emotionally and/or spiritually abusing anyone right now in your life.

- It's not worth it—God sees you
- Remember, you are a child of God.
- You are created in God's image.
- God is not a sex offender or a bully.
- You are hurting another human being.
- You are hurting yourself.
- There is professional help—(mental, emotional, and spiritual).

FROM ME TO YOU

I want to encourage you by saying that no matter what happened to you that you are an overcomer. You are more than a conqueror. You can do anything that you set your mind to do that will make you a better person. Please do not let any type of abuse prevent you from being what God meant for you to be.

I am happy to say that I have grown tremendously in my spiritual and earthly journey. I have attended and graduated from fine schools. I am not done. Whatever God has for me, it is certainly for me. I do not let anyone define me. I cannot be abused spiritually or emotionally because every time someone tries to hurt me, I have learned to give it to God.

There is no greater avenger than God. The enemy might think he is getting over, but no; he is not! Don't worry yourself about looking like a docile lamb; God has given his saints power to overcome the enemy. He puts us in the category of a lion. We have a mighty roar.

> *"The Lord bless you and keep you; the Lord make his face to shine upon you, and be gracious to you; the Lord lift up his countenance upon you, and give you peace" (Numbers 6:24-26)* (NRSV).

Personal Prayers

Personal Prayers

Personal Prayers

Personal Prayers

Motivational Scriptures

Motivational Scriptures

_____

_____

_____

_____

_____

_____

_____

_____

_____

_____

_____

_____

_____

_____

_____

_____

_____

_____

_____

_____

_____

_____

_____

Motivational Scriptures

_____

_____

_____

_____

_____

_____

_____

_____

_____

_____

_____

_____

_____

_____

_____

_____

_____

_____

_____

_____

Motivational Scriptures